P9-BJQ-680

Praise for *Evolutionary Relationships*

"*Evolutionary Relationships* is a vital, indeed magnificent contribution to our conscious evolution. Evolution can be understood as a 13.8 billion year labor of love to create beings who embody love. Yet relating to each other is so challenging that often our yearning to love one another is aborted. Patricia Albere takes us by the hand and guides us through the transformative power of relating, with wisdom and gentle brilliance. It's a major work and essential reading for all of us now."

~ **Barbara Marx Hubbard**, author of *Conscious Evolution, Emergence: The Shift from Ego to Essence,* and *The Hunger of Eve*

"Patricia Albere's *Evolutionary Relationships* opens a transformative lens on relationship that is truly mutual and co-creative. She outlines the intentions and practices that make this frontier possible at a time when new structures for connecting and caring are essential. You'll find yourself nodding, breathing more deeply, and diving in to learn and integrate evolutionary and revolutionary new connections that both nourish and contribute to a new world."

~ **Kathlyn Hendricks**, Ph.D., BC-DMT, author of *Conscious Loving* and *At The Speed Of Life*

"*Evolutionary Relationships* offers a groundbreaking approach to intimacy and mutuality. Deeply personal, but based in thousands of hours of work and collaboration with extraordinary people from all walks of life, Patricia Albere takes us to the upper limits of 'We.' All of us grow best when we have some sense of where we're going, and this book provides not just a vision but an *experience* of the highest possibilities of human relating."

~ **Keith Witt, Ph.D.**, author of *Integral Mindfulness, Shadow Light,* and *Waking Up: Psychotherapy as Art, Spirituality, and Science*

"Patricia Albere hands us the kind of intimacy we have been starving for our whole lives. *Evolutionary Relationships* is a refreshing, enjoyable and innovative guide to a new mutuality that stands to shape humanity for the next millennium. Required reading!"

~ **Rob McNamara**, author of *The Elegant Self* and *Strength to Awaken* with a foreword by Ken Wilber

"Today, a growing number of thinkers are relating to evolution not simply as a scientific theory about the origin of species, but as a lens through which to understand the nature of our complex and fast-changing world. Across the spectrum of science, philosophy, psychology, and spirituality, 'Evolutionaries' are applying this new perspective to a multitude of fields, and Patricia Albere is one of the first to bring it to bear on the dynamics of human relationships. I have no doubt that this book will find a ready audience among those inspired by an evolutionary worldview."

~ **Carter Phipps**, author of *Evolutionaries: Unlocking the Spiritual and Cultural Potential of Science's Greatest Ideas*

"In *Evolutionary Relationships*, Patricia Albere shares a message that impacts not only our personal relationships but the future of our planet. The book illuminates our capacity for a higher order of relating that unleashes the power of love and creativity that inherently exists between us as human beings. Relationships are the threads that weave the social tapestry of the world, and evolving our capacity for relatedness is critical if we are to move beyond the many crises that confront us. This profound yet practical book offers clear advice for creating and developing the kind of relationships that can change ourselves, each other, and our world."

~ **Lynne Twist**, author of *The Soul of Money*

"Meaningful human relationships provide the primary context in which spiritual experience and spiritual growth can occur. This is why it is so important to understand our relationships as forms of spiritual practice. In her insightful book, Patricia Albere shares her practical, proven, and inspiring advice for gaining higher and deeper levels of mutuality with our partners. Her book will help readers find the full spiritual potential of their relationships and fulfill the promise of extraordinary love."

~ **Steve McIntosh**, author of *The Presence of the Infinite*, *Evolution's Purpose*, and *Integral Consciousness*

"In every age there are a few great ones who open new doors of insight, potential, creativity, and joy — new arenas of what is possible. Patricia Albere is one of these people. In the same way personal computers and smartphones opened vast new realms, Patricia's work reveals new forms of relating. I predict this book will change the course of human evolution."

~ **Martin Rutte**, co-author of *Chicken Soup for the Soul at Work*

"Patricia Albere has been conducting basic research into what it is to evolve in mutuality with other people. This book is a report from the frontiers of her explorations. What she has discovered is that love is not just an emotion but an evolutionary force, a force that drives all the fragments of the universe — including us — toward greater connection and wholeness. In this beautifully-written book Patricia shares insights and practices to help you create deeper, more satisfying and fruitful relationships with all the people in your life."

> ~ **Jeff Salzman**, author of *How to Get Results from People* and curator of *The Daily Evolver* online magazine

"Human relationships are not static, but have evolved over the course of history depending on the nature of the human mind in any given era. With the activation of the Ninth Wave of the Mayan calendar system in 2011, entirely new possibilities are emerging for self-transforming relationships from a higher source. Patricia Albere is a pioneer of this field, and in this fascinating book she outlines the mutual awakening which results from such partnerships. She invites us to explore what this emerging self-transformation may come to mean in our own relationships."

> ~ **Carl Johan Calleman, Ph.D.**, author of *The Mayan Calendar*, *The Nine Waves of Creation*, and *The Purposeful Universe*

"Patricia Albere has made the next step in our collective evolution completely clear. This book is a rare combination: It articulates a truly new-paradigm way of relating, but in a completely simple and step-by-step way. It will be of equal interest to change agents seeking to evolve society and couples wanting more depth and intimacy in their relationship. Patricia's techniques are building quickly into a movement — join it now!"

> ~ **Tim Kelley**, author of *True Purpose* and founder of the True Purpose® Institute

"*Evolutionary Relationships* is an ingenious work, transporting us to our innermost essence: Love. Patricia Albere's innovative practices offer us the means to actualize this love-energy in our individual human relationships and expand it to include our world family. Albere echoes the message at the heart of the world's emissaries of love and peace who remind us that we are indeed One."

> ~ **Michael Bernard Beckwith**, author of *Spiritual Liberation* and founder of Agape International Spiritual Center

EVOLUTIONARY RELATIONSHIPS

Unleashing the Power of Mutual Awakening

Patricia Albere

Foreword by
Katherine Woodward Thomas

Oracle Institute Press
Independence, Virginia

Published by Oracle Institute Press, LLC

A division of The Oracle Institute

88 Oracle Way

Independence, VA 24348

www.TheOracleInstitute.org

Copyright © 2017 by Patricia Albere

All rights reserved. No part of this book may be reproduced, transmitted, utilized, or stored in any retrieval system in any form or by any means, including, without limitation, electronic, digital, mechanical, photocopying, or recording, without the prior written permission of Oracle Institute Press.

Publisher's Cataloging-in-Publication Data

Albere, Patricia, author.
    Evolutionary relationships : unleashing the power of mutual awakening/Patricia Albere; foreword by Katherine Woodward Thomas.
        pages cm
        Includes bibliographical references.
        LCCN 2017943530
        ISBN 978-1-937465-23-0 (paperback)
        ISBN 978-1-937465-24-7 (pdf ebook)
        ISBN 978-1-937465-25-4 (mobi ebook)
        ISBN 978-1-937465-26-1 (epub ebook)

    1. Interpersonal relations. 2. Love. 3. Spirituality.   I. Title.

HM1106.A43 2017   158.2
                QBI17-828

Cover Design by Jenene Fusco-Russo
Interior Layout by Diane Dutra
Printed and bound in the United States

DEDICATION

My deepest gratitude goes to my mother. I am one of the fortunate ones who can declare without reservation that I was successfully mothered. My mother had a clear and simple intention to be there for my brother and me. She was psychologically unencumbered, physically healthy, financially safe, and loved and supported by my father. As a result, her attention was free to love and care for us.

It is our birthright as human beings to grow surrounded by real love and support. Maybe that's why I never thought about it, until I walked into a transformational seminar at the age of eighteen and heard people share painful stories of what they had experienced instead.

I never had to "recover" from my mother. Her capacity for true love allowed me to develop naturally and confidently. I know that my ability to be a vehicle for the new intersubjective consciousness explored in this book is a result of her skillful ability to love, which was unconditional, attuned, and effective. Even in the last few years of her life when dementia had set in, my mother loved wholly. I remember once picking her up at the Denver airport. She came toward me in a wheelchair being pushed by an attendant, and upon seeing me she started to clap her hands, raise them to her face, and cry with joy. She spontaneously erupted with happiness that I was her daughter! It's pretty amazing to live on the other end of that kind of support, to know that someone on the planet was thrilled that I exist.

Interestingly, even as her dementia worsened, my mother never forgot family and friends. My mother's love for the people in her life wore deep grooves in her brain. She'd put on crazy combinations of clothes and forget where her room was located, but she never forgot the details or concerns of our lives. After I told her I was writing a book, every time she saw me, she'd ask if the book were finished. She wanted to share it with the people in the nursing home where she lived.

My mother birthed me into this world and taught me how to love wholeheartedly and give without reservation. She never gave me a reason to close my heart. As I held her when she was dying, my heart broke open further … into the vastness of love in which she exists now. No doubt, my mother still is joyfully celebrating my existence and whatever good I might be able to transmit to others through this book. I am forever grateful for the grace of being her daughter.

My second birth came through the love I shared with Peter, my fiancé and eternal beloved. In the four short years we had together before he died, we lived inside a fire of love and illumination that awakened us together. You will come to know Peter as you read this book, because the intensity and power of what Peter and I lived helped create this work. We developed what I now call an "Evolutionary Relationship."

Jalaluddin Rumi famously wrote, "Lovers don't finally meet somewhere, they're in each other all along." Sacred union is eternal, and I now know with absolute certainty that true love is stronger than death. So with all my heart, with everything I am, with everything we are, I dissolve in gratitude.

~ Patricia Albere
June 8, 2017

CONTENTS

FOREWORD

Patricia Albere is five steps ahead of us. Having dedicated decades to awakening the space between us, she now is standing at the summit, peering out intently at a possibility for human relatedness that most of us can't yet quite see, but sense lies just beyond the limits of our own awareness.

Her vision is fresh, compelling, and above all hopeful. For who among us is not restless with the sober conviction that we must find our way to a new level of consciousness if we ever hope to successfully solve the urgent and dire problems we now collectively face? A consciousness where these terrifying challenges can not only be solved, but in many cases, actually outgrown, such that they are no longer even relevant threats.

Those of us who care — *which I'm assuming is all of us who hold this beautiful book in our hands* — are impatient with the knowing that many of our good and noble efforts to address these crises have simply been rearranging deck chairs on the Titanic. Despite more than two thousand years of cultivating our individual spiritual capacities to awaken the Kingdom of God *within* us, it is now the absence of the Kingdom of God *between* us which threatens our very existence.

So many images we have of our future are dark and barren, filled with fighting over scarce resources and dog-eat-dog struggles for survival. Not so the future Patricia offers us. Hers is a deeply benevolent world of harmony, attunement, authenticity, cooperation and kindhearted connection. And if this seems like a pipe dream, it is simply because collectively we still are operating out of the primitive hallucination of separation that prevents the organic emergence of this kind of co-creativity and care between us.

The shift to utopia that so many of us are waiting, hoping, and praying for will not magically materialize one day. This transformation can only happen *through* us, and not just *to* us — through a deliberate step-by-step devotion toward evolving our own skills and capacities in that direction, so that we might become the people we need to become in order to co-create that world.

Those of us on a spiritual path speak of Oneness as the goal for humanity, yet few offer an actual pedagogy for how we might get there. This is where Patricia comes in. She is a master teacher in this new paradigm of relatedness that will allow us to enter the promised land. What makes her teachings so extraordinary is that they are a unique combination of both theory and practice. So many great ideas about where our consciousness needs to go from here are philosophical in nature. Yet Patricia's methods are a means by which we can actually awaken to Oneness through Evolutionary Relationships — the first stage of the "WEvolution" that we are yearning for.

Refreshingly, she presents herself not as a guru who has arrived, but as a seasoned student and an evolutionary leader of this pioneering work, inviting us all along for the ride as she continually clears the pathway toward this new kind of awakening. I see her almost as a camp counselor of consciousness, blowing her whistle as she leads us through the thick of the woods, joyfully declaring, "Hey guys, over here! Come this way!"

Most of us have been devotees of personal and spiritual growth for quite some time. I myself had a spontaneous spiritual awakening at the age of fourteen while visiting the Sunday School class of a girlfriend. From that moment forward, I have organized my life in one way or another around knowing and serving this benevolent Force and field of Life that I've been deeply in love with ever since. Even as a bad-ass kid in high school, I'd sit in the girls' room with my other bad-ass girlfriends, smoking cigarettes, skipping classes, and reading Bible passages to them, with a fierce desire to be of service to their spiritual awakening.

Over the years, my devotion has led me to spend many thousands of hours on both my meditation cushion and a therapist's couch, feeding my deep and cavernous hunger to transform the darkness within myself and awaken to a rich relationship with the beauty and goodness of Life. Yet in all that time, my quest for personal enlightenment — sitting on my meditation cushion to experience the God within — was never as interesting to me as the desire I had to create and compel the emergence of a deeper love between all living beings. It's not that the spiritual path has never included instructions on how to be with one another. Most of us were raised with an awareness of the Golden Rule and Christ's admonishment to love others as we love ourselves. Yet these teachings seem somehow to be a rule book one is meant to follow, as opposed to radically alive practices that would inspire the actual experience of awakening in relationship with others.

For years this confused me, since the only model I saw for true spiritual advancement was of a sole individual sitting with eyes closed in a seeming state of euphoria. Yet the idea that God also could be experienced with eyes wide open and while connected with others has always intrigued and fascinated me. And so, even though I'd always thought myself a bit odd, I stopped judging myself and surrendered to doing what I was driven to do to the best of my ability. Today, I still meditate, but not simply to realize personal enlightenment — now I sit on my cushion to stay centered and strong and to focus on how I can be of service, helping to fulfill the vision of a more deeply related and caring world.

I don't believe I'm alone in being odd in this way. You yourself may be as well, which is why I'm thrilled that we are here together to sit at Patricia's feet! Through *Evolutionary Relationships*, Patricia transmits the vision of mutual awakening with a partner. She also provides the practices we need to develop the potent skills and powerful capacities that move us to the next level of our individual and collective awakening.

I predict that one day soon, we will find ourselves walking down the street, driving in our cars, or sitting on a subway, profoundly related to and organically connected to those around us, whether we know them personally or not. For when enough of us are awake in this way, we then will know how to solve our many unsolvable problems and co-create a world that we will feel proud to pass on to future generations.

~ Katherine Woodward Thomas

Katherine Woodward Thomas, M.A., M.F.T., is the *New York Times* bestselling author of *Conscious Uncoupling: 5 Steps to Living Happily Ever After* and *Calling in "The One": 7 Weeks to Attract the Love of Your Life*. She is a licensed marriage and family therapist and a leading voice in the field of interpersonal relationships. She has taught thousands of people from all corners of the world in her virtual and in-person learning communities.

PART I
MUTUAL AWAKENING
Prologue: The Longing

There is a candle in your heart, ready to be kindled.
There is a void in your soul, ready to be filled.
You feel it, don't you?
You feel the separation from the Beloved …

~ Rumi

I was sitting in my kitchen when "it" awoke. My two-year-old son, in his blue plastic chair, was sitting beside me eating his lunch. Below my window, the well-worn cobblestones of our tranquil Milanese courtyard soaked up the midday sun. The city was quiet, doors closed, while people gathered for lunch and a moment of repose before returning to work.

Then out of nowhere it came. I felt the most intense longing arise within me. It was like a tornado unexpectedly appearing in the midst of a clear day, tearing through the countryside and rearranging the landscape. My heart and then my whole body started to burn with intensity. It seemed to force its way into my awareness, cracking through the surface of my contented life, leaving me aching with an inexplicable, inconvenient, overwhelming desire for love. I wanted to love and be loved — *passionately, deeply, and completely* — but in a way I had never considered.

The love I was longing for was not a love I had ever known, not the delicious thrill of romance or the companionable parallel paths of my married life. I wanted to dissolve and die into something far greater. And I could sense that it wanted me too. What I longed for had no face or name. Was it a person? Was it my deeper self? Was it God? I didn't know. What I did know was that it was so vivid and real that beside it my life seemed pale and insubstantial.

Have you ever experienced a longing like that — a restless, mysterious, undeniable sense that something is missing and calling you? Are there moments in the midst of your busy life when you feel the ache of a deep loneliness, even though there are people all around you? Do you sometimes feel like you're missing something or someone, but you can't quite say what or who?

Many people have told me that they've had this kind of experience. Even those who lead successful, fulfilling lives surrounded by friends and loved ones can inexplicably find themselves filled with a yearning for something more, a sort of "divine discontent." Suddenly, this longing arises, sometimes as a gentle, nagging discomfort, other times as a searing desire.

When this longing first arose in my awareness, it shocked me and woke me up. I was fearful, apprehensive, but also fascinated. As a successful, married woman living a stable, comfortable life with my husband and young son, I didn't want to admit (even to myself) how much I yearned for a deeper and more compelling experience of love and consciousness. I didn't know how to find what I was seeking or if it really existed. I didn't even know what it was that was flirting with me. Consequently, allowing myself to feel the longing was the greatest risk of my life. But I let it in anyway, let it fill my awareness, and allowed it to swing like a wrecking ball through my comfortable life and leave me standing in the rubble … defenseless, excited, and facing the unknown. I allowed myself, as Rumi wrote, to "be silently drawn by the pull of what you really love."[1]

Most of us are afraid to feel this deep longing because we don't know why it is calling us or what it is asking us to do. We want to satisfy our existential hunger, but we fear that by opening ourselves up to it, we may subject ourselves to a life of fairytales and frustration. Nevertheless, when I opened my heart to this sacred longing, I found it had the power to transform and transfigure me. Such fulfillment truly is possible, and some of us are capable of integrating this evolutionary impulse that calls us to a new order of love and relating — what I call "Evolutionary Relationships."

After my marriage disintegrated — taking with it my family's approval, my reputation, my community, and many of my friends — I had nothing left to hold on to but this divine longing. So I let it lead me on an improbable journey, signposted by intuitions and coincidences, until I found myself visiting a large and soon-to-be infamous spiritual community in Oregon. There, I met an unusually awake, mystical man named Peter, who would reach into my soul and change my life forever. From the moment Peter and I met, something was set in motion that we couldn't control. It was as though the pattern of our oneness already existed, engraved in the fabric of the cosmos, just waiting for us to stop resisting its gravitational pull.

When the spiritual community imploded in a much-publicized scandal just a few weeks after we met, Peter and I reluctantly separated, but the intensity of my need to be with him soon overwhelmed me. Real love is shattering in a most magnificent way: destroying ideas, plans, and all our unconscious inner structures that create separation. True love is relentlessly humbling, reducing our defenses, displaying our vulnerabilities, and evoking an unambivalent "yes" to life. As a result, within a few short months, Peter and I found a way to be together, allowing our mutual longing to penetrate layers of falseness, insecurities, fears, and separateness. There were times when, lying in his arms, I found myself crying from pure relief — a total surrender to what I had been trying to find my entire life. With ultimate wonder, I began to understand what the longing was pulling me toward. It wasn't just Peter; it was what our coupling revealed to me about the true purpose and potential of human relationships. Peter and I had entered into a state of "mutually awakening," a spiritual state shared by two people, which I now realize is part of a larger movement of consciousness.

Today, many people are moving beyond solo spirituality and hyper-individualism into the truth of our interconnectedness. Ultimately, I see humans moving toward a "WEvolution" — a futuristic concept that we will touch on in this book as we explore Evolutionary Relationships, which represent the first stage of this collective awakening.

But it all starts with love. We sometimes forget that love is the most powerful force in existence. Popular culture has tended to reduce it to romance, desire or affection, and while those are some of love's expressions, the force itself is much greater and more mysterious. Philosophers, mystics, and poets throughout the ages have understood and honored the power of love — its potential to draw us deeper and its ability to make us stronger and more courageous. This longing for sacred love unveils what some have called "the Beloved" and others call God. It is no accident that many mystics chose the language of human love and desire to describe their longing for divine union with the evolutionary impulse.

For example, in the 13th Century, medieval German mystic Mechthild of Magdeburg wrote in her *Meditations*:

> God tells the soul, "I desired you before the world began. I desire you now as you desire me. And where the desires of two come together, there love is perfected."
> And the soul replies, "Lord, you are my Lover, My longing."[2]

And in the 16th Century, Spanish mystic Teresa of Avila wrote:

> Since my Beloved is for me and I am for my Beloved, who will be able to separate and extinguish two fires so enkindled? It would amount to laboring in vain, for the two fires have become one.[3]

Rumi, of course, addressed many of his impassioned poems to "the Beloved." For these early mystics, the Beloved was not a person. In fact, for most mystics even today, the longing for union draws them away from the society of people. Alone in the desert or on a mountaintop, they seek oneness with God and more easily find the Beloved in solitude.

But how much more exciting to discover the Beloved in the form of another human being! At this moment in history, many of us have had a peak experience, touched bliss, and tasted oneness. Moreover, I believe this potential is now emerging for more and more of us at the frontier of human development. We have evolved from divinely *inspired* to divinely *inherent* human beings, who now have access to the process of mutually awakening with others.

> *People are starting to awaken together, both in paired relationships and in community collectives. The resulting Evolutionary Relationships are still rare but growing in number, as the field of the WEvolution beckons us …*

In the years Peter and I spent together, we experienced the divine love that Rumi wrote about. We existed not as two individuals but as a unified field — sensuous, fluid, and flowing. We were capable of feeling each other's feelings and knowing each other's thoughts before and as they arose. Effortlessly, we entered higher states of consciousness and were shown greater dimensions of love and reality. Yet, this book is not about our love story. It's about what I gained from my first Evolutionary Relationship, and what it taught me about the extraordinary potential for a higher order of human relatedness.

Since receiving the precious gift of an Evolutionary Relationship with Peter, my life has been devoted to helping others activate this possibility for mutual and collective awakening. Over the past few decades, I've worked with thousands of men and women, and this book shares what I've learned about how to create a new kind of relatedness that fulfills our deepest longing for love, intimacy, and sacred union.

Evolutionary Relationships are not limited to romantic partnerships. You can create one with a close friend, with a colleague, and even among a group of people, so long as each individual feels the same divine longing and is willing to surrender to its irresistible pull and commit to its fulfillment. Today, Evolutionary Relationships represent the unfolding edge of our development as a human species. In truth, the longing is not *our desire for divine love* so much as *divine love desiring and needing us.* This new dimension of love and more evolved consciousness needs our surrender and our wholehearted cooperation.

If this book has found its way into your hands, I hope that what you find here will speak powerfully to you. I trust it will make you feel clearer, more inspired, and more empowered in your own sense of what is important — that which is needed and worth fighting for, living for, and giving to generously. This book, after all, is about LOVE. The early 20th Century Jesuit mystic Pierre Teilhard de Chardin put it this way:

> *The day will come when, after harnessing space, the winds, the tides and gravitation, we shall harness for God the energies of love. And on that day, for the second time in the history of the world, we shall have discovered fire.*[4]

I believe that day is close at hand, and this book is intended to hasten its arrival. This book also proves our capacity as human beings to love each other and enter into a shared consciousness of unity, which does indeed harness the energy of love for something higher than ourselves. And in the process, we will come to know ourselves more distinctly, while at the same time feeling our interconnectivity with others in Evolutionary Relationships.

New forms of connection are arising in the outer world, and I believe we need to develop new forms of consciousness between us that inform how we relate collectively. Just as the internet has brought us ever closer, we need to create an "innernet" that reflects the higher values of shared awakened consciousness. In fact, the force of evolution is pushing us to access the deep unified field of our interconnectedness and to experience this field as our normal way of knowing ourselves and each other. We are a transitional generation, moving from an older form of human being to a new modality — from *homo sapiens* to what some are now calling *homo universalis.*

I am a teacher and spiritual practitioner, but above all, I consider myself an artist. My medium is consciousness and the life force, as it manifests through me and through the people with whom I have the privilege of working. This book is the expression of my art — the fruition of forty years of living, teaching, and working intimately with thousands of people. My teachings are not a fixed or finished product, but a continuing emergence, which I have done my best to capture on these pages as it is presenting itself at this moment in time.

Today, I continue this critical work in a group called the Evolutionary Collective. Many of the stories contained in this book come from members of this group. As such, these stories constitute a secondary experience of and engagement with evolutionary potentials. Knowing "about" something and understanding it mentally can be interesting and even fascinating, but my intention is to give you direct access to this new dimension of consciousness. I want you to be able to taste it, know it, and live it for yourself, discovering how it shows up in your life and in your relationships, so that when it does, you'll feel the excitement of being a vehicle for the WEvolution of love.

As you read this book, I encourage you to embrace the ideas and perspectives I'll be sharing. Allow these concepts to create a new context for your life, even if they confuse you, disturb the status quo, inspire agonizing longings, or open you to mind-blowing possibilities. The more you engage experientially with this book, the more you will experience the transformative power of love in your own relationships.

For decades as a student of spiritual wisdom, I immersed myself in books and benefited from master teachers. Now, as a teacher myself, it is clear to me that in order for people to truly transform, they need to integrate new material in three distinct ways, but depending on your natural tendencies, you may favor just one of these learning styles.

First, you may be the type of person who seeks cognitive under-standing. You may prefer to read books, take courses, and listen to the recordings afterward to gain additional knowledge. You may take notes and enjoy discussing various perspectives with other students. Second, you may be the type of student who follows an experiential approach to learning. You may like to immerse yourself in practice and don't particularly care about information that contextualizes what you are experiencing. Or third, you may be the type of person who wants to take action and apply what is being learned to implement change. Neither understanding nor having a deep experience is your priority. Rather, your focus is practical and action-oriented.

As a teacher, I know that if a person unconsciously follows their natural learning tendency, they likely will grow in a distorted way. For example, you might gather more and more information, or accumulate more and more experiences, or take action without the proper depth of understanding or spiritual maturity. Therefore, this book provides the necessary ingredients for balanced growth. I'll be sharing information, experiences, and tools for taking action. Most importantly, I'll be offering you the opportunity to create Evolutionary Relationships in your life.

My suggestion is that you read through the book once and allow it to expand and inspire you. Then, go through the book again and work with the exercises. There are practices that you can do alone with a journal and ones that will require a partner. Chapter 3 will assist you in choosing the right partner for this work and instruct you on how to approach the exercises together. Lastly, if you would like to connect with others who are exploring these same potentials or wish to explore additional resources for your journey, please visit my website: **www.EvolutionaryCollective.com**.

What in your life is calling you when all the noise is silenced …
The meetings adjourned, the lists laid aside,
And the Wild Iris blooms by itself in the dark forest ...
What still pulls on your soul?

In the silence between your heartbeats hides a summons.
Do you hear it?
Name it, if you must, or leave it nameless,
But why pretend it is not there?

~ Terma Collective[5]

Notes

1   Rumi, quoted by Larry Chang, *Wisdom for the Soul: Five Millennia of Prescriptions for Spiritual Healing*, Washington, DC: Gnosophia Publishers, 2006.

2   Quoted by Henry L. Carrigan, Jr., editor, *Meditations from Mechthild of Magdeburg*, Brewster, MA: Paraclete Press, 1999.

3   Translated by Kieran Kavanaugh and Otilio Rodriguez, *The Collected Works of Saint Teresa of Avila*, Volume Two, Washington, DC: ICS Publications, 1980.

4   Pierre Teilhard de Chardin, "The Evolution of Chastity" (February 1934), in *Toward the Future*, translated by René Hague, New York, NY: Harcourt Brace Jovanovich, 1975, p. 87.

5   Terma Collective, "The Box: Remembering the Gift," quoted by Sheri Gaynor, *Creative Awakenings: Envisioning the Life of Your Dreams Through Art*, Los Angeles, CA: New Insights Press, 2009.

CHAPTER ONE
What Is an Evolutionary Relationship?

*There are vast realms of consciousness still undreamed of –
vast ranges of experience, like the humming of unseen harps ...
a marvelous rich world of contact and sheer fluid beauty
and fearless face-to-face awareness of now-naked life.*

~ D.H. Lawrence, *Terra Incognita*

One winter evening, I fell in love at New York's Carnegie Hall. I was sitting in the front row, applauding with almost three thousand others as the virtuoso cellist Yo Yo Ma took to the stage, accompanied by the great vocalist Bobby McFerrin. I knew the collaboration between these two musical giants would be something unique, but I could not have anticipated the experience I would have that night.

From the outset, the love and respect that these two performers had for each other was palpable. It seemed to bounce back and forth between them, flowing like the music itself, weaving a field of irrepressible joy that rippled out from the stage. At one point, a draft caught the set list that lay on the floor and it fluttered off the stage and fell at my feet. I bent forward to pick it up and hand it to them, and as I did so, they playfully drew me into their field, as though my outstretched hand holding the piece of paper was another instrument joining in the spontaneous harmony they were creating. I felt lifted up on a wave of creativity and ecstasy that compares to the experience of falling in love. Indeed, it seemed as though the whole auditorium was falling in love, not with any particular person but with the joyful energy that was pulsing amongst us. With each new burst of musical brilliance, the performers inspired and uplifted each other, and with each wave of applause and laughter, the audience embraced them, until it felt like there was no longer a stage separating us, but simply one unbroken field of love and happiness delighting in itself. *This is what's possible for human beings* — I thought — *how human relatedness can be.*

There are seven billion people living on planet Earth, and by 2050, there will be more than nine billion. Our sheer numbers and our communication technologies are bringing us ever closer, connecting each one of us to a web of relatedness like nothing the world has seen before. Thirty-nine percent of humanity has access to the internet, and by some estimates, more than ninety percent have mobile phones. The mass uprisings of the Arab Spring were made possible by tools like Twitter, allowing vast numbers of people to communicate and self-organize. Using our social networks, we're constantly coming up with innovative ways to coexist and share resources in our ever-more-crowded world — from the "city bikes" that recently appeared outside my New York City apartment, to the rise of "couch surfing" websites like Airbnb, to car-sharing schemes and so on. We truly are living in an age of interconnectedness.

Interestingly, there is a parallel trend that's been noticed by some spiritual teachers and luminaries with whom I've worked. They have observed that around the turn of the millennium, as internet use became more widespread and the "world wide web" of connectivity intensified, spiritual awakening became available more naturally to individuals and collectives as well. Experiences like the one I had at Carnegie Hall were occurring among groups of spiritual practitioners, often spontaneously, sometimes consciously generated. Mystics of old described visions of a Global Awakening, where the multitude of connections between us would "light up" with love and creativity. For example, Sufi mystic Llewellyn Vaughan-Lee writes:

> *A web of light has been created around the world to help us make this transition. Through this web the invisible is already becoming visible, the signs of God already revealing themselves in a new way. In the energy of divine oneness the opposites have already come together. But love needs us to bring this potential into manifestation, to make it part of the fabric of daily life. Without our participation the potential will ebb into a fading promise of something that might have happened.*[1]

And he expands on the implications of this idea:

> *If that light can be brought into consciousness, then it can travel through the web of connections, awakening centers of consciousness within all of humanity. Humanity will have access to the wisdom, power, and love that it needs to take the next step in its spiritual evolution: to learn to function in oneness, as a dynamic, interrelated whole. Without this awakening, patterns of energy-flow around the planet will remain dormant, or function on a lower level, and once again humanity will have missed an opportunity.*[2]

Many contemporary thinkers hearken back to the early 20th Century visionary Pierre Teilhard de Chardin, who had written about the "Noosphere" — the network of collective human thought that envelops the planet just like the biosphere — which he believed would intensify and complexify as evolution continued. We now are seeing evidence of what he foretold. Terms like "collective consciousness," "co-intelligence," and "synergy" are becoming more common. Even some progressive business leaders have started experimenting with ways to ignite the collective intelligence and creativity of their teams.

By the 1990's, I started to feel restless. I'd been working as a teacher while studying intensively, immersed in two spiritual paths and reading the work of great masters and psychological visionaries. Essentially, I felt unsettled working on my own and with other people's *individual* spiritual development. Something else was awakening and wanted to express itself through me — a slow burning fire that had been sparked back in those years with Peter. It had been more than a decade since Peter's death, and I wanted to rekindle the heightened shared consciousness I had shared with him, the level of awareness that can emerge in the field between people. I felt a calling to work with people who had come to the same realization regarding their personal spiritual development. So I began to work with others who were ready to awaken *collectively*.

> *My calling is to hold open the portal to a new dimension of love and joy that only emerges in the field between people who are committed to new and deeper forms of intimacy.*

Today, the need for deeper and more authentic forms of relating is urgent. Paradoxically, despite our ever-increasing connectedness and glimpses into our collective potentials, many of us feel more isolated than ever before. According to a recent survey, thirty-five percent of Americans over age forty-five are "chronically lonely."[3] Young people grow up online with hundreds of virtual friends, but as a recent *New York Times* story put it, technology allows them to "end up hiding from one another, even as [they] are constantly connected to one another." The author, MIT Professor Sherry Turkle, laments that we have left behind the "rich, messy, and demanding" world of human relationships for a "cleaned-up" world of technology-enabled connection.[4] Similarly, a recent cover story in *The Atlantic* entitled "Is Facebook Making Us Lonely?" echoes Turkle's concerns, concluding that our "web of connections [has] grown broader but shallower."[5]

The internet — an infrastructure of connection — is here and growing, but now we need to balance it with the "innernet" — a new kind of relatedness that has the power to burst the bubble of lonely, alienated individuality that so many of us live in, along with the power to ignite an awakened field of consciousness within which groups of people may coexist and prosper. The moment has come for us to pursue what the mystics describe. By turning our attention toward collective forms of development and awakening, we may light up the pathways between us with more vibrant energy, love, and creativity. We must learn to unite in a much deeper and more profound way if we are to successfully navigate the challenges presented by our globalizing world. In sum, we are capable of creating and enjoying a more interconnected and fulfilled reality.

A New Frontier

It's been my observation over four decades of teaching that even the most highly developed and spiritually enlightened human beings don't necessarily know how to have deep, intimate, and transformative relationships. Often, we spend years developing ourselves, yet still feel frustrated with our relationships, intuitively knowing that more should be transpiring when we come together with others. We sense that something beautiful is possible between human beings, yet too often we find ourselves struggling and compromising in order to just "get along."

Moreover, we tend to assume that highly evolved individuals spontaneously attain highly evolved relationships. But for the most part, this is not the case. Just because two musicians are virtuosos doesn't mean they will be able to spontaneously and harmoniously play together, like Bobby McFerrin and Yo Yo Ma did that night. The same goes for the spiritual giants among us, and I know a story that perfectly illustrates this point.

One of my friends had the privilege of being invited to a special gathering of some of the world's most revered spiritual teachers, including His Holiness the Dalai Lama and Depak Chopra. My friend was humbled and honored to be in the presence of so many radiant and luminous souls, spiritual leaders who inspire thousands, if not millions around the world. One might assume that getting a group of people together of that caliber would ensure a powerful emergence of something new, and that the meeting would have a transformational impact of some kind on the world. Nevertheless, my friend was disappointed by the gathering. Speakers took turns expounding their own wisdom (and some were deeply inspiring), but no new way of being together collectively occurred. Nothing new was created. It was like a group of great soloists playing one after the other, but never becoming an orchestra.

My friend's story has stayed with me because it demonstrates so clearly that individual spiritual development does not automatically translate into an awakened way of being together or collective transformation. It's not due to the fault or failing of individuals; it's simply that the space between us is not awake yet. That space represents a different dimension of awakening and that's where our focus needs to be. Our individual awakening is not enough, nor will it allow us to move into humanity's next era of connectedness — an era that must be founded on the reality of unity.

Consequently, it is critical that we begin to learn new ways of relating, that we begin to pay attention to the space between us and what can be birthed by a heightened connectivity. If our most enlightened leaders don't naturally find new ways to relate to each other in a manner that brings forth enhanced connections, love, and creativity, then what chance do our governments, businesses, or families have to bring forth a new domain of relatedness?

Personally, I am convinced that if we wish to move to the next stage of our spiritual and cultural evolution — what I call the "WEvolution" — those of us who are fortunate enough to devote significant time and energy to our personal growth must now learn to relate to each other in a dramatically new way. To clarify: I am not simply referring to a relationship where love, acceptance, and freedom from judgment exist — the virtuous ideals modeled for us by our wisest spiritual teachers. Rather, I mean a unique form of relationship which fosters an interpenetrating depth and which calls forth each person's true potential within a fertile, co-creative field.

I've often compared this deeper form of relating to the moment when single-cell life forms divided to became multi-cellular organism. Then, DNA was exchanged through reproduction and creativity was completely unleashed, resulting in even grander combinations of life. Similarly, when humans come together in an Evolutionary Relationship, they cross the divide of separation, witness new potentials, and attain a new quality of consciousness that only may be shared with others.

In this type of relationship, we are inspired, touched, moved, excited, and creatively ignited by each other on a daily, if not momentary basis — just as those two great musicians were made greater by their mutual love and respect. A whole new frontier of human development opens up when we turn our attention toward the space between us — the "vast realms of consciousness still undreamed of," according to D.H. Lawrence. This new dimension of relatedness — whether it emerges with a spouse, a lover, a colleague, close friend, or family member — becomes nothing less than a dynamic engine for mutual evolution and global creativity.

> *An Evolutionary Relationship is a consciously created connection that is formed between two or more people who mutually commit to explore and develop higher states of perception and awareness together.*

Since first glimpsing these potentials in my relationship with Peter more than two decades ago, I've dedicated myself to understanding this dynamic, interpreting it, and translating it so that others can consciously create what I've come to call an "Evolutionary Relationship." An Evolutionary Relationship is a consciously created connection that is formed around an explicit mutual commitment to developing higher potentials, individually and together.

An Evolutionary Relationship doesn't just benefit the individuals involved — it becomes a vehicle for bringing new potentials alive at the leading edge of human evolution. This kind of relating allows us to move into a more fluid, interdependent, and interconnected consciousness, where each person's essential uniqueness and the experience of unity can coexist. This mutually awakened state is so dramatically different from conventional connections that it represents a paradigm shift. Therefore, such relationships are inherently *evolutionary* — opening a door to the next stage of our collective human development.

I have had the unique privilege to work with thousands of men and women over the years, and I've witnessed a vast spectrum of human relationships, from the most basic, primitive, utilitarian kinds of connection, to the indescribably refined, exquisite experiences of unity. As a result, I've come to understand that not every relationship has the potential to be an evolutionary one. That doesn't mean that the relationships you have are not beautiful and valuable, but it's important to know the difference. Each relationship has innate potentials. We can't choose what those potentials are, but we can open ourselves to discover what is possible and then fully activate that particular relationship. It's like blending colors: If you have red and blue, you have the potential to make purple, but if you try to make green you will experience frustration. However, you can blend red and blue to make a deep purple — the most magnificent purple possible.

Some relationships have ceilings,
while others have skylights that open
to cosmic realms you may never
have dreamed existed ...

Sometimes when we experience disappointment in a relationship, it's not because we're with the wrong person but because we don't know how to recognize or reach the relationship's potential or how to activate that potential together. Regrettably, some relationships do have a limited or specific ceiling, while others have skylights that open to cosmic realms you may never have dreamed existed. This later type of relationship is what we will focus on in this book — the kind I found with Peter. These Evolutionary Relationships are vehicles for mutual spiritual awakening.

Understanding Human Relationships

Since first tasting this new kind of relatedness, I've been convinced, intuitively, that it represents something more than a powerful experience for just two individuals. I believe it is intimately connected to the next stage of our evolution as a culture and as a species. This belief has led me to study the work of many developmental psychologists, evolutionary theorists, and social scientists — scholars who seek to understand how the potentials I glimpsed might fit into their maps of human and cultural development.

While every map or model has limitations, I've found that by studying and contemplating the distinctions between different levels and stages of human consciousness, the experience of relationship has become more advanced, more potent. For this reason, let's take a moment to reflect on a few of the thought-leaders whose work has been illuminating for me and for many others. My hope is that a brief review of seminal studies conducted by acknowledged philosophers, psychologists, and sociologists will help us place the relationship potentials in the context of our larger human journey.

The early 20th Century psychologist Abraham Maslow created a very useful and widely cited model for understanding human needs. While you may have encountered Maslow's model — called the "Hierarchy of Needs" — you may not have considered how it sheds light on our relationships. I've found it to be very helpful in this regard.

Maslow's model represented human needs as a pyramid: Our most basic survival needs are at the bottom; followed by safety needs; then the need for love, affection and belonging; thereafter the need for self-esteem; and finally the need for self-actualization. Late in his life, Maslow added one more level at the peak of the pyramid — the need for self-transcendence.

The great insight of Maslow's model is the assertion that lower-level "deficiency" needs generally must be fulfilled before the individual can become concerned with higher level "being" needs. According to Maslow, "A hungry man may willingly surrender his need for self-respect in order to stay alive, but once he can feed, shelter, and clothe himself, he becomes likely to seek higher needs."[6] This same lower-to-higher level need satiation pattern arises within the lens of human relationships.

So let's take a closer look at Maslow's model and how it translates into human relationships. If we exist at a survival level — concerned about food, water, shelter, and self-defense — our relationships will reflect those fundamental needs. We will come together with others to help each other survive, and what we will share is the everyday business of fulfilling our most basic needs.

Sadly, many millions of people around the world are living at this survival level today, either due to a scarcity of resources or because of a disaster that has reduced their living conditions to basic survival. Yet, all relationships have to successfully meet this base standard of care in order for us to have the freedom to achieve the next stage of connectedness. Often, we don't realize just how much of our energy is focused on the "logistics" of life — our homes, food, clothing, procreation, and sleep — and these core needs limit the potential of our relationships.

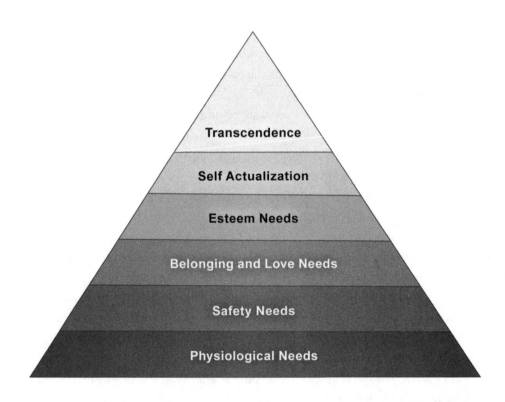

The second level of needs, according to Maslow, is safety, which includes security, order, and stability. Once we handle the basics of survival, we begin to be concerned with securing the skills and resources needed to establish a safe and protected haven. It's fairly easy to see this level of needs playing out in relationships, where we also need to feel physically and emotionally safe. Boundaries, stability, a sense of order, and agreements that keep us safe and create a degree of trust are important for our relationships at this developmental stage. Indeed, trust is crucial for safety. Similarly, if trust and safety are lost in a relationship, the relationship slides backward to the survival level and once again is reduced to logistics.

However, once a safe foundation is established, our energy is free to move onto the next level of desires — love, affection, and belonging. At this stage, we want to feel accepted by others and be part of a family or group. This is when new questions arise: *Do you like me? Do you want me? Do you love me? Am I lovable and desirable?* Belonging is important, and we start to be more focused on sharing common interests, goals, beliefs, political views, and favorite activities. These objectives are less relevant when we're preoccupied with survival and safety, but once we're feeling secure, we have time and energy to pursue interests and goals that create a stronger sense of belonging and give rise to heightened intimacy.

The next level of longing in Maslow's model is esteem. Esteem needs include feeling valued and respected by others. Consequently, in relationships organized around esteem needs, we want to be seen, acknowledged, and appreciated. We want our gifts and talents to be affirmed, our contributions to the world respected, and our gifts and talents affirmed. At this stage, we are naturally drawn to others who have skills and abilities that reflect their own self-esteem and feelings of worthiness. In relationships at this level, we assume additional obligations and play out certain roles. We work together and help each other with resources and connections to create a more complex, successful, and networked life. It's quite different than the utilitarian function of survival or safety-based relationships. Then, once our self-esteem needs are met, we discover new needs surfacing. Having power, prestige, status, respect, achievement, and our value affirmed no longer compels us. Now, we're awakening to the next level of needs, which Maslow called self-actualization.

For an individual, self-actualization marks a new stage of existence. No longer are we concerned with what Maslow defined as "deficiency" needs (i.e., needs inspired by the lack of something). Instead, the desire for self-actualization comes from a sense of fullness, after all of our lower-level needs are satiated and we are free to start asking: *What am I here to contribute? How can I express my true purpose?* Maslow described self-actualization needs as "man's desire for self-fulfillment, namely the tendency for him to become actually what he is potentially: to become everything one is capable of being." Expanding on this sentiment, Maslow continues, "A musician *must* make music, an artist *must* paint, a poet *must* write if he is to be ultimately at peace with himself. What a man can be, he must be." [Emphasis added][7] Similarly, in relationships at this level, we are less concerned with what we can *get*, and more focused on what we are able to *give*. We want to share, to express and contribute, to commit ourselves to developing and maximizing our potentials. Mastery and abundance are naturally present at this level.

Conversely, at the lower levels, despite how much we may care for others, there still is a subtle (or not-so-subtle) neediness within us. Only at the self-actualization level does the force of love release and relieve us from self-concern and the potential I call an Evolutionary Relationship can begin to come into being. Self-actualization gives us the true autonomy required to open and give ourselves more deeply to each other, to risk venturing into unknown territories of intimacy and creativity.

Lastly, the highest level of needs — which Maslow added toward the end of his life and which still is absent from many versions of his model in common use today — is the longing for self-transcendence. Maslow discovered that some people who reach the self-actualization level seek what he called "peak experiences," which he defined as profound and life-changing moments of love, bliss, unity, or divine understanding. For these "transcenders," as Maslow termed them, peak experiences connect them to something greater than themselves and become an overriding objective. In a landmark 1969 article, "Theory Z," Maslow speculated on the qualities of such people, observing that they are more likely to be interested in a "cause beyond their own skin,"[8] and more apt to be innovators, discoverers, and seekers of new approaches in all disciplines.

When we achieve the capacity to love wholeheartedly and without inner conflict, we access higher potentials that allow Evolutionary Relationships.

Self-transcendence is the desire to experience, unite with, and serve that which is beyond the individual self. It is at this stage of development that evolutionary relating can flower. Maslow hinted at this when he noted a quality he called "post-ambivalence," which he described as "total wholehearted and unconflicted love, acceptance, … rather than the more usual mixture of love and hate that passes for 'love' or friendship or sexuality or authority or power, etc."[9] It is this capacity to be able to love wholeheartedly and without inner conflict that releases the higher potential in Evolutionary Relationships. Such a deep embrace of relatedness only occurs when individuals mature beyond all lower-level deficiency needs and establish a ground of being that incorporates self-confidence, self-acceptance, and true self-actualization.

As human beings, we have needs at every level of Maslow's pyramid, so it's important that we have relationships that fulfill us at each level. Therefore, this is not a matter of some relationships being "better" than others, since all of them are important. Just as Maslow's pyramid is smaller at the top, the number of relationships at the highest level naturally will be smaller too. Yet, because Evolutionary Relationships are so intensely transformative, having even one such connection will change your life irrevocably.

In truth, Evolutionary Relationships are rare and only become possible at higher stages of development — stages that only a small percentage of human beings have reached. Many of us are familiar with the research which maps the stages of childhood development, but few people know that pioneering researchers also have mapped the stages through which adults progress. And while some people object to the very idea of such stages, concerned that it promotes elitism or discrimination, those who study evolution argue that this simply is how development occurs — in stages. Understanding the stages through which adult humans progress provides important insight into how we can continue to evolve, both in order to actualize our own potential and to meet the needs of our complex evolving world.

Evolutionary Relationships represent a unique form of relating and require two or more people who individually have reached Maslow's highest levels: self-actualization & self-transcendence.

One of the most respected researchers in the field of adult development is Harvard psychologist Robert Kegan, whose work also provides context for Evolutionary Relationships. In his book *The Evolving Self,* Kegan observes that most human beings progress through a series of five stages of increasing mental complexity and social maturity, which he terms "orders of mind." The first two orders — which most people pass through during childhood — are called the "impulsive mind" and the "instrumental mind." In both these stages, the child is largely self-absorbed.

Next, humans move into adolescence and early adulthood, at which time we develop what Kegan calls the "socialized mind." At this stage of our development, we are heavily influenced by the culture around us, by social norms and expectations. Then, most of us progress to what he calls "self-authoring mind," which Kegan defines as a stage of greater autonomy guided by our inner authority. We now are self-directing and self-defining. If you are the type of person who values independence and resists being overly influenced by others, then you have reached this "self-authoring" stage.

Kegan's research illuminates yet a fifth and further level of development beyond self-authoring, which he calls the "self-transforming mind." Kegan eloquently describes the experience of subjectivity that the self-transforming mind is capable of experiencing — the "interpenetrability of self-systems" and "the interpenetration of self and other."[10] Likewise, Rob McNamara, who is a professor of developmental psychology, discusses the self-transforming mind at length in his book *The Elegant Self.* McNamara writes that at this level of development, "We find a self that can discover its truth and identity in response to and in relationship with an ongoing interpenetrating experiential flux …. This larger intimacy informs a self that is more flexible, dynamic, responsive, and open to a broader, ongoing information flow."[11]

People at this level of development can handle more intense and intimate experiences and they are more naturally attuned to what I will call the "space between." Here, boundaries become less defined and awareness arises from the flow and flux of relatedness. There is a perception of one's distinctiveness, but simultaneously there is an attunement to the interpenetrating experiential flow of connectedness with others.

In sum, most of the qualities Kegan ascribes to the "self-transforming" level of consciousness are resonant with my theory on Evolutionary Relationships. I believe this points to the possibility that this new kind of relatedness is an integral component of the next step in our collective evolutionary journey. It does not negate our independence or individuality, which was achieved during an earlier, critical stage of the journey. However, in order to attain a more advanced level of selfhood, we must be willing to grow even more …

It is important to note that adult development is *not* a guaranteed path. Indeed, research shows that most adults will remain at the socialized and self-authoring levels of development their entire lives. Therefore, those of us who have reached higher levels of emotional, psychological, and spiritual development need to commit to discovering and consciously developing the next level of human consciousness. Remember: Evolutionary Relationships are rare, and if you've been fortunate enough to experience this blissful and creative connectedness, then you know how precious and important the self-transcending level of relatedness is for yourself and for the world.

The Energy of Love

Love is expressed by humans at all levels of development. However, what my observation and research suggests is that Evolutionary Relationships fully emerge only when human beings progress beyond "deficiency" needs in Maslow's hierarchy and enter the realm of the "self-transforming" mind in Kegan's model. Consequently, when a person expresses love from a higher state of consciousness (i.e., beyond neediness and lack), that love manifests differently. Similarly, when individuals no longer bother to conform to "socialized" norms or worry over "self-authoring" individualism, they are free to meet each other in an entirely different manner, and the relationship they form no longer is about two separate people trying to meet each other across the "space between." Instead they experience being intimately inside of a shared experience, inhabiting the same world.

When this level of exploration occurs, you still feel your own distinctness and particularity — in fact, you feel more intimate with your own depths than ever before. But you also feel the other person from inside *their* experience. It may sound strange, but the separation disappears; somehow you are inside each other and feel connected to something that is bigger than both of you, as though your connection with each other is a portal to all of existence. The energy of this vast sharing starts to flow through you and between you, carrying you forward with its own momentum. You feel a yearning that seems to come from the heart of the cosmos — a longing to be related to and express your love for each other and for life itself.

Love is much more than an emotion. It is an evolutionary force that drives the entire cosmos in a never-ending, unfolding process. "Love is the most universal, the most tremendous and the most mystical of cosmic forces," wrote Teilhard de Chardin. "Love is a sacred reserve of energy; it is like the blood of spiritual evolution."[12] Yes, love strives — through human beings — to form higher connections. As Teilhard beautifully put it, "Driven by the forces of love, the fragments of the world seek each other so that the world may come to being."[13] I love this description, as it speaks deeply to my own experience. When we surrender to the force of love and discover this higher level of relatedness, we feel radiant and connected not just to another person but to all of existence. We also feel that the universe is becoming more whole through our unity with each other.

From a spiritual perspective, we can view the evolution of the cosmos as being driven by the forces of love and creativity. While you won't find this perspective in any scientific text, scientists concede that matter and consciousness display an unmistakable tendency toward innovation and more complex forms of life. Furthermore, many respected philosophers, theologians, and mystics have described this underlying force, drive, and impulse in the same way. For example, early 20th Century French philosopher and Nobel laureate Henri Bergson wrote about the *elan vital* (vital impulse), which he defined as "an internal push that has carried life, by more and more complex forms, to higher and higher destinies."[14]

Modern theosophists agree and they posit a new theory of God — no longer an old man in the sky, but the driving force behind evolution. Contemporary spiritual teacher Andrew Cohen calls it "the evolutionary impulse," while A.H. Almaas uses the term "optimizing force." I use both of these terms interchangeably, captivated by the notion that this evolutionary impulse also has the characteristic of moving humanity toward higher and greater expressions of relatedness. Cohen offers a mystical explanation of this cosmic dance in his book *Evolutionary Enlightenment:*

> *[R]elatedness is the whole point of the manifest world. The universe was created so that relationship could occur. ... Before the big bang, in that empty ground, there was only unbroken Oneness. But that One chose to become the many, and in the birth of the many, relatedness became the very fabric of the emerging universe. Indeed, one way to understand the evolutionary impulse is as a desire for perfect relatedness — an overwhelming urge to make manifest its ultimate nature as seamless unity in the realm of multiplicity. ... That's why you feel drawn to others — because the evolutionary impulse is drawn to itself.[15]*

I find the above passage a resonant explanation for the powerful longing I've experienced. But you don't have to venture into such metaphysical realms to understand that the evolution of life tends toward relatedness. Scientists, too, have been following this evolutionary thread. Over the past few decades, researchers have discovered how critical interrelationships are to the evolutionary process. In 1967, Biologist Lynn Margulis shocked the scientific establishment when she published a landmark paper proposing that cooperation, not competition, was the major driver for evolutionary advancement. Margulis was not studying humans or even the animal kingdom; she was probing the microcosmic realm of bacteria. Since that time, others have expanded on her research and observed the same principles at work in all forms of life. My good friend Carter Phipps describes this scientific trend in his book *Evolutionaries:*

> *This new wave of science looks at the evolutionary process from stem to stern and sees marvelous example after marvelous example of cooperation and sociality in the service of evolution. ... The evolutionary advantage goes to those most capable of good teamwork and most willing to engage in the kind of cooperation that turns a collective of individuals into something more than the sum of its parts.*[16]

Thus, whether we're dealing with bacteria coming together to form the first cell, cells coming together to form organs, or living creatures coming together in cooperative cultures, the desire to unite appears to be intrinsic to the evolutionary process. Moreover, scientists like Margulis, Elisabet Sahtouris, and others are describing in biological terms the same process that Teilhard was describing when he wrote that the "fragments of the world" seek each other out. Scholar and theologian Beatrice Bruteau sums up Teilhard's vision eloquently:

> *In Teilhard's view, all of evolution has progressed by a series of creative unions. More complex and more conscious beings are formed by the union of less complex and less conscious elements with one another. Subatomic particles unite to form atoms, atoms unite to form molecules, molecules unite to form cells, and cells unite to form organisms. This same pattern of creating something new, something more complex and more conscious, by the union of the less complex and less conscious recurs at each of these levels. It is because we can look back and see the pattern, see it recurring, that Teilhard believes we can legitimately extrapolate and project the pattern into the future, looking forward to another creative union in which we will be the uniting elements.*[17]

Together, we can create a channel for the evolutionary impulse to work its magic at a new level of complexity and consciousness. When relating to others in this way, we feel a new energy activated or awakened within us and between us — a volcanic surge of love and intentionality that bubbles up and erupts as we let it express itself through our Evolutionary Relationship. The vulnerability and beauty of such intimacy is quite delicate, often sensuous, and at times almost unbearable. There is a cosmic creativity in this kind of love, a unique power that is released when we become consciously close and transparent, when we feel the other as our self.

Evolutionary Relationships dissolve the separation between us, allowing us to access a unified field where together we may channel cosmic creativity and contribute new gifts to the world.

Historically, there are examples of people experiencing heightened consciousness and peak experiences through the ancient *tantra* tradition (i.e., divine sexual union), which still is practiced today. However, an Evolutionary Relationship does not require a sexual partner, even though that is one powerful form of its expression. What is distinct in this work is that you can experience an Evolutionary Relationship with a friend with whom you have a deep spiritual alignment and want to create or work together. It even can happen with someone you've just met, provided you're both committed to the same kind of potentials in the relationship.

Recently, during one of my workshops, I saw a beautiful example of two people developing an Evolutionary Relationship. Students were randomly paired up and asked to work on exercises that would activate higher potentials. One woman, Sharon, was paired with Tim, a man she didn't know very well. As they began the work together, she was shocked to experience a powerful intimacy and connection with this virtual stranger.

"It was refreshing to experience that depth of intimacy without a marriage certificate!" she told me afterward. Tim also remarked on the closeness they experienced. "I told her, 'I think I love you,'" he remembered, "and she said, 'that's inevitable.'" The kind of love that Sharon and Tim experienced had nothing to do with romantic attachment. Nevertheless, Tim said, "It made me a little uncomfortable at first. Even though there was nothing romantic or sexual happening, it almost felt wrong to be so intimate with someone else's wife." Later, he met Sharon's husband, who joined a subsequent workshop, and Tim was amazed to have a similar experience with Sharon's husband!

By practicing these principles, another man who attended one of my workshops experienced such closeness with strangers that he was able to identify the "gap" — that which was lacking in his relationship with his wife. He was so excited during the final session because he couldn't wait to get home and share what he had discovered with her.

I have shared profound Evolutionary Relationships with a number of people I work with at the Evolutionary Collective. The journey together is awakening new potentials in all of us, and we constantly are amazed by its power, beauty, and capacity to activate these potentials for the many others who work with us. When we approach each other in the ways that you will learn in this book, the potentials that emerge between us as human beings are rich and full and surprisingly powerful. I call these friends and colleagues my "multiple beloveds." As we explore the space between us, we "fall in love" — collectively — and we discover new depths of connection. That love is latent in all relationships, just waiting to be activated.

In the chapters that follow, I will be sharing the practices and disciplines I've developed which will allow you to begin developing your capacity to create Evolutionary Relationships. This may mean that you take an already meaningful relationship and expand that relationship with an increased potential for mutual awakening. It may mean that you attract someone new into your life who is ready for this kind of relating. And while there may be only one or two relationships in your life that are truly evolutionary, the Mutual Awakening Practice contained in Chapter Three of this book will affect all of your other relationships as well. Your heightened sensitivity, intuition, empathy, and love will naturally impact everyone with whom you connect.

The time has come to affirm what your heart is seeking … longing for … ready for. Do you feel the mystery calling you? If you have the courage to explore mutual awakening, you will be amazed at the degree of intimacy, vulnerability, beauty, and connection that is possible with another person. I invite you to join me inside the surging, emerging evolutionary impulse and discover where it can take us, together.

CONTEMPLATION:
What Are Your Relationships Based On?

Take a moment to consider one or two of the most significant relationships in your life, then ask yourself: *What are these relationships really organized around?* Without any judgment, just observe whether and how these relationships meet: (i) your survival needs; (ii) your safety needs; (iii) your need for belonging, love, and care; and (iv) your need for esteem. Are there aspects of any of those needs that aren't being addressed? Are any of your relationships meeting the higher needs for self-actualization and self-transcendence? Here are some questions that will help you shed light on your relationships:

- ⌘ What roles do you play?
- ⌘ What roles does the other person play?
- ⌘ What expectations do you have of the relationship?
- ⌘ What do you want and need from the other?
- ⌘ What does the other want and need from you?
- ⌘ How do you think the other sees you?
- ⌘ How do you see the other?
- ⌘ Who are you in his/her eyes?
- ⌘ Who is he/she for you?
- ⌘ What do you see as the full potential of this relationship?

(continued on next page)

When answering these questions, you probably will find that many of your relationships are organized around the lower level needs in Maslow's hierarchy — the "deficiency" needs. This may include your family, certain friends, and perhaps an ex-husband, wife, or lover. In such relationships, we tend to unconsciously fall into particular roles.

For example, one person may represent authority and the other rebellion, or one person may act weak and helpless so the other person can take the role of the caregiver or white knight. Especially in co-dependent relationships, there is little intention to grow, develop, or create anything more out of the connection and we remain unconscious of what else might be shared. As mentioned earlier, relationships have a nature and purpose all their own. However, when we become more conscious of what is transpiring in our relationships, we sow the seeds of greater development.

On the other hand, you may observe that some of your relationships are organized around self-actualization needs — the people with whom you share common interests and passions. These might include close friends, lovers, or colleagues at work. In this kind of relationship, you enjoy richer interactions, deeper sharing, and stronger support. Additionally, your way of relating is more conscious and therefore more satisfying, nurturing, and fruitful.

If you're lucky, there may be some relationships in your life that are organized around what Maslow called self-transcendence. In such relationships, people commit to growing and evolving together and creating something larger and more significant than either person's individual needs. In fact, you may feel that you have some greater destiny with each other! So there's a totally different level of dedication and interaction that can transform both of your lives. This is what I would call an Evolutionary Relationship. It's a higher order of relating that activates and supports both of your highest potentials, brings you into a different state of consciousness, and contributes to the greater good of humanity. ෨

For supplementary content, including audios, videos, and exercises, visit: www.EvolutionaryRelationshipsBook.com/bonus

Notes

1   Llewellyn Vaughan-Lee, "The Web of Light," *Light of Consciousness Journal*, Spring and Summer 2003.

2   Llewellyn Vaughan-Lee, "Working with Oneness," http://www. workingwithoneness.org/articles/working-oneness.

3   AARP Survey, 2010, cited in Stephen Marche, "Is Facebook Making Us Lonely?" *The Atlantic*, May 2012.

4   Sherry Turkle, "The Flight From Conversation," *The New York Times Sunday Review*, April 12, 2012.

5   Stephen Marche, "Is Facebook Making Us Lonely?" *The Atlantic*, May 2012.

6   Quoted in Edward Hoffman, *The Right to Be Human: A Biography of Abraham Maslow*, New York, NY: McGraw-Hill, 1999, p. 143.

7   Abraham Maslow, *Motivation and Personality*, New York, NY: Harper and Row, 1954, p. 9.

8   Abraham Maslow, "Theory Z," http://maslow.org/sub/theoryz.php.

9   Ibid.

10   Robert Kegan, *In Over Our Heads: The Mental Demands of Modern Life*, Cambridge, MA: Harvard University Press, 1994, p. 315.

11   Rob McNamara, *The Elegant Self: A Radical Approach to Personal Evolution for Greater Influence In Life*, Boulder, CO: Performance Integral, 2013, p. 78.

12   Pierre Teilhard de Chardin, *Human Energy*, New York, NY: Harcourt Brace Jovanovich, 1971, p. 34.

13   Pierre Teilhard de Chardin, *The Phenomenon of Man*, Toronto: Harper Perennial Modern Classics, 2008, p. 264-5.

14   Henri Bergson, *Creative Evolution*, New York, NY: Henry Holt and Company, 1911, p. 102.

15   Andrew Cohen, *Evolutionary Enlightenment: A New Path to Spiritual Awakening*, New York, NY: SelectBooks, 2011, p. 196.

16   Carter Phipps, *Evolutionaries: Unlocking the Spiritual and Cultural Potential of Science's Greatest Idea*, New York, NY: Harper Perennial, 2012, p. 83.

17   Beatrice Bruteau, "A Song that Goes On Singing," interview by Amy Edelstein and Ellen Daly, *What Is Enlightenment?* Spring/Summer 2002, p. 55.

CHAPTER TWO
Awakening to the We

We are one, after all, you and I.
Together we suffer, together exist, and
forever will recreate each other.

~ Pierre Teilhard de Chardin

Samuel and Paula had been happily married for eight years. They lived in a beautiful apartment in San Francisco with their three small children, all under the age of six. When they came to one of my recent workshops, however, their marriage was visibly strained. They felt like they'd done nothing but fight the past few months, as they juggled two careers, children, and a busy social calendar. They'd seen a therapist and were trying to be more accommodating of each other's needs, but felt unable to recapture the kind of easy togetherness they'd once experienced.

Samuel was familiar with my teachings and hoped that if Paula joined him at my workshop, maybe they could find a solution to their problems. I asked the couple to do a practice that began with simply sitting together, being present, and then answering — one at a time and with vulnerability — the question: *What am I experiencing?*

Once they had spent a few minutes with this exercise, I asked them to turn their attention to a different question: *What are WE experiencing?* With short words and phrases, they took turns answering this question, which required that they pay attention not to their own internal thoughts and feelings, but to something else, something between them, that place where their consciousness overlapped.

After they'd been doing this practice for about ten minutes, I looked at Samuel and Paula and noticed that they appeared more relaxed and open. In fact, their faces were lit up with a sweetness that I palpably could feel, and it was obvious that they had connected in a deep way. I asked Paula what transpired, and she said, "I feel like I just found our relationship again! All these months, I thought we were working on our relationship, but in fact we were just two separate people working on ourselves or trying to change each other. We had lost touch with the place between us, the place where our connection and our love exists."

As Paula and Samuel continued to engage in the workshop practices, they didn't "fix" their problems. Instead, many of them just naturally seemed to fall away, and the couple had a bigger place to come from in dealing with those that didn't. They weren't trying to change themselves or each other anymore. Rather, they were developing and delighting in the living connection between them, and out of that space, they were finding creative ways to navigate their complex lives. More importantly, however, as Paula and Samuel rediscovered how potent their connection was, they became less and less concerned about working on their "issues." As a result, they felt much more inspired to find out what new potentials could emerge between them.

The We-Space

What Paula and Samuel's story illustrates is the most critical shift we need to make if we're interested in pursuing higher potentials of relatedness. They shifted their attention to the place where relatedness exists — the space *between* us, where we overlap and our consciousness intermingles. Most people do not pay attention to that space between us or "we-space," but it's a very real and important part of human interaction. In philosophical terms, it's called the "intersubjective" domain.

We're all familiar with the concept of "subjective" experience, which often is defined as the inner, personal, and private world that each of us lives on a momentary basis. Most of us also are familiar with the "objective" domain, which is the scientifically measurable world of objects that each of us observe and largely can agree upon.

Yet, the intersubjective domain is different: It is the shared space of consciousness that exists between two or more people. This intersubjective field is more than simply the sum of two or more individuals in communication. Because relationships have an existence of their own — an "ontological reality" as philosopher Steve McIntosh calls it[1] — this realm has its own "being." It's a shared reality where we are in full contact with the same interior experience. The current paradigm assumes that because our bodies are separate, our consciousness is distinct as well. But we've all experienced moments (if not steady states) of oneness, of being inside the same experience, *together*. Some examples of this state include love, compassion, joy, laughter, penetrating clarity, and a myriad of other experiences.

What is new about this approach to relatedness is that we consciously focus on awakening to the space between us. Rather than communicating across the distance between two bodies and two subjective realties, we are placing our consciousness "inside" the other and focus on the "we" that arises when we are in a state of true communion.

This we-space doesn't just arise in our most intimate relationships. It's a field of invisible yet powerful connectedness that we move into and which takes on different qualities when we relate to different people. Every relationship has an intersubjective dimension that reflects particular qualities and characteristics. It can be stagnant, negative or toxic, or it can be alive, dynamic, transformative and thriving. Imagine the difference between the field generated by a creative team that is brainstorming and creating a novel, world-changing idea, and the quality of the field produced by an angry, drunken mob. Consider the contrast between the vibration of an excited crowd at a football game, and the energetic frequency of a church congregation. Now, it's easy to see how the intersubjective field of relationships and groups invisibly shapes what can and can't happen for the people who are a part of it. Indeed, I believe that this field shapes the group experience just as much as our surface interactions shape it. However, most people remain unconscious of this field and sadly miss the amazing potentials that can be accessed.

The "we-space" that resides within the intersubjective domain constitutes a shared reality where two or more people are in full contact with the same interior experience.

The fact that most people are unaware of this field of interconnectedness does not make it any less real. As Dr. Martin Luther King, Jr. wrote, "We are tied together in a single garment of destiny, caught in an inescapable network of mutuality."[2] Throughout the ages and across the spectrum of traditions, spiritual teachers like Dr. King have told us the same thing: *At the deepest level, we are all one and everything in this world is interdependent.* Paradoxically, this underlying oneness gives rise to the multiple unique forms in which we find ourselves. Yet, our essential nature is unity — with each other and with all of life.

Recently, science has begun to confirm this theory. Ecologists have shown us the miraculous and fragile interdependence of our planetary systems — summed up beautifully by the great naturalist John Muir, who wrote, "When we try to pick out anything by itself, we find that it is bound fast by a thousand invisible cords that cannot be broken, to everything in the universe."[3] Quantum physicists have explained to us that our world is not made up of pieces of matter but of dynamic systems of energy that exist in a constant exchange of information with each other. As author and researcher Lynne McTaggart explains in *The Bond:*

> *Between the smallest particles of our being, between our body and our environment, between ourselves and all of the people with whom we are in contact, between every member of every societal cluster, there is a Bond — a connection so integral and profound*

that there is no longer a clear demarcation between the end of one thing and the beginning of another. The world essentially operates not through the activity of individual things but in the connection between them — in a sense, in the space between things.[4]

As we go about our day-to-day life, we tend to be unaware of what McTaggart calls "the Bond" — our deeper connection to each other and the cosmos. We hear about oneness, we read the insights of the mystics and the breakthroughs of the scientists, but then we perceive ourselves as separate objects, bumping into each other. Like Paula and Samuel, we're often out of touch with the we-space, even in our closest relationships. Our automatic locus of awareness is ourselves and we live inside a bubble of self-concern. As a result, it takes practice and humility to penetrate the membrane of separation.

Becoming aware of the "we" immediately changes the way people relate to each other. For example, an elementary school teacher named Joan who has been working with me shared that she has seen the power of we-space among her young students. She found that when she introduces the concept of oneness to a classroom of eight-year-olds, their behavior shifts. "I remember one particular little boy," she recalled, "who stubbornly refused to follow directions. I said to him, 'Instead of arguing about whether you'll do this assignment your way or my way, how about we figure out how to do it *our* way.' He totally understood and let go of his position. We figured out together — from inside the 'we' — what was best for both of us." Joan has used this concept in her classroom for years now, and she reports that it has turned the teacher-student relationship into a "creative partnership."

Sometimes, an unexpected event shifts the intersubjective field, suddenly making us notice the we-space that previously had been absent from our awareness. After the tragic events of September 11, 2001, I heard many stories of such sudden shifts. I was teaching in New York City shortly after 9/11, and one of my students, a woman who lived on the Upper East Side, told me that as she walked around her neighborhood immediately following the tragedy, she noticed that everyone on the sidewalks seemed to be inside a shared consciousness, and people spoke more freely with one another. She said she felt connected to complete strangers in a surprising new way and that it seemed perfectly natural to be open and trusting with her fellow New

Yorkers. Similarly, a male New York resident told me that no horns were honked for several days after the towers fell. The city was unusually quiet, and there was a natural flow of cooperation and compassion that clearly was unusual for Manhattan.

Yet, the most powerful description of the post 9/11 we-space came from Tom, a man I know who is an emergency medical physician and head of a New York nonprofit. Tom regularly flies into places like Haiti to deal with the aftermath of disasters. Normally, when he arrives at a strange hospital there is an immediate resistance from the staff members, who vie for position and express other aspects of ego. But when Tom went downtown to help with the 9/11 rescue, he said there was an unexpected openness and holistic connection that allowed everyone to work together in a flow of efficiency that he's never experienced since. He said that he and his trauma teammates moved and responded as one organism.

It seems to me that it was the shock of 9/11 which awakened people. Residents of New York City suddenly became connected inside a field of relating that is very different than the reality in which we normally exist. They shared an unusual level of openness and vulnerability. Imagine if the consciousness of New York could have remained inside that level of connectedness, flow, and love for not just a few days, but for a year or more?

The shock of 9/11 created a powerful we-space. People broke through and accessed an empathetic and authentic field of relating that was beautiful to witness and evident to all!

I am passionate about teaching the underlying principles that will allow human beings to relate from that kind of connection and concern for one another, and I am not the only one. My colleague Andrew Venezia in his paper "I, We, All" writes, "Many of our crises today as a global humanity stem from our inability to interface and relate with each other, in small and large scopes, from such a [we-space]. Our technological sophistication has outstripped our ability to create beauty and goodness."[5]

We fail to reach this level of relating partly due to cultural pressures. In the United States over the past half-century, our culture has encouraged an increasingly individualistic worldview. However, some of us also have been taught to follow our hearts and sense of purpose, to resist bowing to convention, to create healthy boundaries and also respect the boundaries of those we love. This is a positive and important cultural development, but it is not enough. Now, we need to find the courage to move beyond our separate spheres of enhanced individuality, to connect more deeply, and to awaken the sensitivities necessary for collective evolution. As we begin to pay attention to the "intersubjective" dimension of our experience, we will discover how to be in relationship not just with each other, but with the "we" and our greater humanity.

We also fail to reach this level of relating because our awareness generally is focused on the gross level, that which appears to be solid and material and separated in space. As we pay attention and become more sensitized to the intersubjective field, we begin to experience more subtle levels of consciousness that permit us to sense the invisible realms of reality such as subtle energies, inner sounds, visions, smells, tastes, and touch. When this unseen relational field awakens, we become more alive, more vivid, more dimensionally rich. This we-space is vibrant and expansive, and it reveals deeper levels of reality.

Who Is Relating?

The potential for Evolutionary Relationship emerges when two or more people become aware of the field between them and when the field becomes aware of itself. Just as an individual can become "self-aware," so too can this "we-space" become conscious of itself ... but only if we become conscious of it, *together*. But before I can explain how to activate this extraordinary potential for an awakened "we," there's one more critical question we need to explore.

Relationships are affected by many factors, but one of the most important components is: *Who is doing the relating?* Spiritual work is always a matter of identity. The great mystics reached enlightenment by asking the question: *Who am I?* And anyone who has done even a little psychological or spiritual work will be familiar with the notion that there is more than one of us "in there." Though there are many ways of describing the different dimensions of the self, for the purposes of creating an Evolutionary Relationship, we need to focus on two particular dimensions: the first I will call the "ego-self," and the second, the "essential self."

The ego can be described as our fixed sense of identity that we develop in childhood through our relationships with other people and the environment. Our sense of self begins to form around self-images that are fixed, repetitive, limited, and familiar. Through the experiences of our childhood, the structures of our ego develop and provide us with an every-day sense of self-recognition. The ego's fixed and repetitive nature gives us a stable sense of self — a center from which to live and engage with the world. The ego also is experienced as a platform for constant inner activity: thinking, feeling, hoping, planning, ceaselessly reinforcing and validating our sense of self. Fundamentally, the ego is a closed system that works to maintain itself. By seeing our habitual ways of being and doing, we realize the ego is repetitive and almost mechanistic.

On the other hand, the essential self is the experience of being free from external reference points. It is a sense of self that does not depend on self-images, ideas, feelings, sensations, hopes, or fixed impressions. Rather, it is self-existent, which means it is not conditioned by our parents, our education, or our culturally adaptive qualities or characteristics. The essential self is our true self, the sense of identity which arises from our core essence.

The essential self is a sense of being
that originates from Source.
It is our true nature, and it is deeper than
our current experience in this incarnation.

Thus, the essential self represents our true nature, making it deeper than the history of our current incarnation. It's the face that we had before we were born. If we had a different body, different name, or different sex, it's who we are and who we are seen and known to be by those who love us best. Indeed, the people who truly love us recognize what I call the "origination point." Each of us has an origination point, a point of light that comes from the source of our existence, which radiates into the world and expresses itself in the form of our particular life.

Often it is easier to recognize the origination point in others. Just think about someone whom you've deeply loved over time. Contemplate that person's indefinable and unique essence — what you love about him or her. Your relatedness to that person comes from a place you may not fully recognize, yet you are drawn to this person irrevocably, by a distinct and mysterious sense of mutual attraction.

Now, imagine being in touch with your own origination point or essential nature. It is a space that feels like home. Your essential self also should feel dynamic, since it is an open system and a field of consciousness that evolves, grows, and constantly exchanges information with the cosmos. Consequently, your essential self is not stagnant. It is capable of developing new structures that contain greater consciousness and complexity, and it integrates and releases old structures as needed. Others sense when you are alive at this level of spiritual maturity, when you are ready, willing, and able to dissolve old ego structures that limit or compromise your essential nature.

Here are some more clues to help you unveil your essential nature. As your sense of identity shifts from ego to essence, you will experience a sense of being natural and free. You feel like you are effortlessly yourself— authentic, distinct, and unique. You find you no longer draw comparisons between yourself and others, nor are you trying to be "someone." When in touch with your origination point, your sense of self flows naturally and unselfconsciously.

Lastly, I wish to underscore that the essential self is impressionable, always morphing and changing, fluid and flexible. Thus, the experience of living from essence is one of discovering who we are at our core and who we are evolving and maturing to be. I have a student I've worked with for over twenty years who now is eighty-seven years old. She is an artist in New York City and she is radiant, delighting in her life and in herself. She managed to release her soul from her ego long ago, and she will be evolving until her last moment on Earth. She's an inspiration to me, as she demonstrates that being alive and growing has nothing to do with the body or aging process. Conversely, some people only identify with their ego and stop growing early in life. When we identify with the fixed qualities of our ego, we settle for a closed system and we experience entropy and disintegration. Old age only applies to the ego. The essential self is an open system that endlessly evolves.

Awakening Mutuality

The field of relatedness has been described by many philosophers, physicists, sociologists, and mystics, but I particularly like the one-word definition offered by Dr. King: *mutuality*. In ordinary usage, mutuality connotes reciprocity, sharing, partnership, and mutual benefit. In my work, I use it to refer to that place where souls overlap — a confluence of consciousness. Mutuality also points to the fact that relationship is a two-way street, where two or more individuals agree to be consciously related.

Unfortunately, many relationships suffer from lack of real mutuality, with one person using the other person to fulfill his or her own wants and needs. As previously explained, when we relate from our egos, we unconsciously see others as separate, as images, as objects of desire, protection, help, advancement, comfort, and so forth. Generally speaking, most relationships are an interplay of separate people interacting and exchanging, but never really communing or entering into the depth of union I am pointing to. That's because ego identity always filters: it creates a particular image of the self and a particular image of the other, and it is those two images that come together rather than our essential selves. When I use the term self-image, I don't just mean a visual picture of the self. It's a solid and compelling sense of self, more akin to a virtual reality. It's a sense of self that is informed by our senses and subjective observation, all of which seems perfectly normal.

For example, if my self-image tells me I'm small and delicate and need protection and support, whereas my partner is seen as big and strong, then these two images will connect together in a powerful attachment. It may seem like a great relationship, but in actuality it is just two self-images fitting neatly together. No real contact is occurring between this couple, and the relationship will work only so long as neither one sees through the illusions of ego, which probably were developed in childhood. When our relationships are based on these types of superficial and unexamined images, there is no real or authentic exchange. The relationship initially may feel stable, but eventually the stagnation and lack of true contact will make it difficult for this connection to be sustained, particularly if one of the partners starts to awaken.

Again, mutuality emerges when two or more people occupy the same space in consciousness. As Sufi scholar Kabir Helminski writes, "Two stones cannot occupy the same space, but two fragrances can."[6] Truly, our souls are more akin to fragrances than stones because they are permeable, able to commingle without losing their essence or their autonomy, while our egos always remain separate, like two stones tumbling in the ocean of consciousness but never blending with it.

However, once we access mutuality with a partner, we start to contact the relationship itself, like Paula and Samuel achieved. When starting from a place of deeper unity, we bypass the clash of wills, ulterior motive, and hidden agendas. We are awake and present and honestly see each other. We can tune in and listen to what the relationship itself desires, what it's ready for, and what potential it contains. Then, if we want those potentials to be fulfilled, we can elect to work together to expand and deepen our experience of mutuality. What I call "evolutionary mutuality" is a true union of souls, in which there is an unbounded merging of the essential self of both individuals, who each remain distinct and unique but who achieve a heightened state of awareness and engage in dynamic interplay.

Mutual awakening starts with moving beyond our separate sense of self into full and immediate contact with our essential nature. Only then, may we come into reality with another. Once we become aware of our inner essence in all its fullness, the next stage is to connect with the inner experience of the other. When this is achieved by both partners, a sacred space is created where the partners become aware of the field of relatedness between them. At the final stage, we may access multi-dimensional awareness, which means we simultaneously become aware of self, other, the space of relatedness, and often many other different dimensions as well.

Evolutionary mutuality starts
with both partners locating and merging
their essential natures. Thereafter, a true
union of souls may occur, one in which
cosmic co-creation is possible.

Mutual awakening is the process of coming into reality together. Instead of autonomically focusing on our individual, subjective world, we lean toward each other, into the "space between" and discover our innate unity and capacity to be inside reality as one. We find that reality is dimensionally rich and layered. Science has accepted that hidden dimensions and unseen realms make up a greater portion of the universe than the physical, visible elements. The surprising gift is that when we practice mutual awakening, we not only develop a quality of consciousness that is more fluid and intimate, we simultaneously become aware of different dimensions. This multi-dimensional awareness allows us to move beyond a separate sense of self into full and immediate contact with our own distinct and essential nature, while also experiencing the essence of the other and together entering into an awakened consciousness. This field is enlivened by our presence, and we are enlivened by it. Our shared consciousness is a portal to unlimited potentials and often, extraordinary experiences that take us beyond realities we previously have known.

Mutual awakening can occur with more than two people, but it only comes into existence when a group pays attention to the space between them within the greater field. When we meet others beyond the separation of egoic consciousness, something miraculous happens. We fall through the rabbit hole into a deeper, always present reality that is dynamic and alive. Love permeates everything and creativity abounds.

By learning to let go and enter this field together, we awaken simultaneously — it's never just happening to one person. This is an entirely different process than the kind of individual awakening that has been described for thousands of years by spiritual mystics, with their myriad techniques and practices. Instead, mutual awakening is an invitation to become something greater together, though spirit. What's exciting is how available it is, as though consciousness itself has been waiting for us to pay attention in the right way. When we do pay attention, we experience the mystical depths of shared unity, and we shift our normal way of being and acting in the world.

Mutual awakening is the first stage of the WEvolution — a movement of attraction and expansion between two or more people who wish to give and receive at higher and higher levels. The more energy is exchanged, the more mutuality occurs. This reciprocity of energy, attention, and love creates access to unending dynamism and new evolutionary potentials. In this heightened state, Evolutionary Relationships serve as channels for our connection to each other and to the greater intelligence and energy of the cosmos, the universal mystery and greater reality to which all of us are connected. As the Bible states, "Where two or three have gathered together in My name, I am there in their midst."[7]

Notes

1   Carter Phipps, *Evolutionaries: Unlocking the Spiritual and Cultural Potential of Science's Greatest Idea*, New York, NY: Harper Perennial, 2012, p. 169.

2   Dr. Martin Luther King Jr., "Letter from a Birmingham Jail," 1963, Stanford University Martin Luther King, Jr. Research and Education Institute, https://kinginstitute.stanford.edu/king-papers/documents/letter-birmingham-jail.

3   Stephen Fox, *John Muir and His Legacy: The American Conservation Movement*, Boston, MA: Little, Brown and Company, 1981, p. 291.

4   Lynn McTaggart, *The Bond: Connecting Through the Space Between Us*, New York, NY: Atria Books, 2012, pp. xxiv-xxv.

5   Andrew Venezia, "I, We, All: Intersubjectivity and We Space, Post-Metaphysics, and Human Becoming," 2013, http://studylib.net/doc/9722222/venezia-i-we-all, p. 60.

6   Kabir Edmund Helminski, *Living Presence: A Sufi Way to Mindfulness & the Essential Self*, New York: NY: TarcherPerigee, 1992, p. 130.

7   Matthew 18:20, New American Standard Bible.

CHAPTER THREE
Practicing Mutual Awakening

When you make the two, one
and when you make the inner as the outer and the above as below,
and when you make the male and the female into a single one,
then you shall enter the Kingdom.

~ The Gospel of Thomas

When Peter and I were together, we never used a particular technique to generate the intense experience of mutuality that we shared. We simply surrendered to each other and to the relationship, by following whatever was unfolding between us. In this way, we were led to ever-greater heights of openness, intimacy, presence, and transformation. Maintaining a continuous sense of connectedness was our way of being together, and the thought of developing a "practice" out of our shared experience never occurred to me. The intensity of love and the desire to be as close as possible was what motivated us.

After I lost Peter, I was left in the confusing and painful position of carrying our shared awakening alone. He was gone, and yet I still felt our ongoing connection. Eventually, after a period of intense grieving, I was driven to understand what had happened to me and felt the need to recreate the same depth of mutuality in my life with others. So I began a deep examination of my experience with Peter to truly discover what had made our dual awakening possible.

I spent many years studying with various teachers, driven by these questions: *How do I give people access to this powerful and catalytic dimension of consciousness? How do I share it and enter into it again with others?* Eventually, I discovered how to recreate the experience. I found myself able to use simple exercises that would consistently give people access to this kind of mutuality.

Today, I have identified "Eight Activating Principles" that help us turn toward each other and catalyze this unique consciousness. Through the remainder of this book, I will be sharing these principles, so that you can experiment with others to achieve mutual awakening. To start, I'll share a foundational practice that I used with Paula and Samuel and thousands of others to awaken this deeper dimension of relatedness.

Are You Ready for an Evolutionary Relationship?

I'm sure that many people reading this book have deep and loving relationships, and maybe you have glimpsed the kind of potential I've been describing with a lover or a friend. Perhaps you've had "peak" experiences but never considered that you could share that elevated consciousness with another person. Or maybe you've never had that experience, but some part of you has always yearned for it.

You also may be in a relationship that has grown stale, or perhaps you feel trapped in an unhappy marriage. This book is not intended to help you "fix" a damaged relationship — there are many other wonderful teachers and counselors who can help in such cases. But for those of you who are ready to consciously create something new with a partner or friend who shares that intention, this book will show you how you can develop and open yourself to the extraordinary potentials that are awaiting you in this new domain of relatedness.

Additionally, this book will help you activate the evolutionary potential for higher relatedness by introducing you to powerful practices and principles for catalyzing deeper connectedness. This doesn't mean you can force the process or that you'll be able to predict how it will unfold. The process includes a mysterious element, which neither you nor I can control. For example, I did not "manifest" Peter in my life, with all the miraculous joy, wisdom, and awakening he brought. But I did make myself "available" for the sort of relationship that Peter offered, by listening to my deepest longing, by letting my desire take me into places I had never gone before, and by opening my heart to possibilities I had never dared let myself consider.

Recently a friend and spiritual scholar told me about a Sufi practice of ecstatic communion called *sohbet*. In the Sufi tradition, there are three ways to access the divine: prayer, meditation, and *sohbet*, with *sohbet* considered the most powerful method. Although the practice is described in different ways — with some claiming that language is inadequate to capture its subtlety — *sohbet* often is defined as "companionship in conversation." This type of communion relies on ancient, oral traditions. Through storytelling, mystical love and knowledge is shared between practitioners, "in such a way that it attempts to circumvent the knots of the rational mind and connect the hearts of the seekers. *Sohbet* can be understood as a spiritual dialogue, a cleansing of the soul and a meeting of the hearts."[1]

Scholar Olga Louchakova describes *sohbet* as a heart-to-heart dialogue. She explains, "The lived experience of participants in the *sohbet* is treated as an alive body of emerging sacred text, consciousness in the process of becoming. It is a sincere, kind, conscious conversation around meaningful and essential issues ... among people having no operating defenses or power agendas."[2]

I like to imagine that *sohbet* is what Rumi and his mentor Shams shared — a spiritual transmission of divine love, which utterly transforms and unites both people. Long after Peter died, I read Rumi's poetry, in which he agonizingly longs for his Beloved. For the first time, I felt someone understood my pain and the depth of my loss, and I was fascinated to learn that Peter and Rumi shared the same birthday. Although I've never practiced *sohbet*, I feel a strong connection with this ancient tradition, as it seems closely aligned in spirit with the practice I call mutual awakening.

Finding the Right Partner

Because it is impossible to experience mutual awakening by yourself, to get the most out of this book, you will need a partner. Moreover, many of the exercises I'll be sharing are designed to be done by two people, so I highly recommend that you find a partner with whom you feel comfortable exploring the concept of mutual awakening. At this point in the book, perhaps someone already has come to mind — a close friend, a lover, or even a new connection — someone you know who also is interested in these potentials. If so, I suggest you talk to that person and ask him or her to read the book with you. Then, you can move through the practices together.

Often, people hesitate when trying something new. We wait to be invited and fail to create an opening for engagement and participation. This book is about a new domain of consciousness that is rare, still new, and mostly unexplored. So you will need to be the inviter and the innovator. You will need to extend yourself by approaching someone first and assuming the risk and the difficulty of sharing something novel with that person. Some of your friends may not be ready, but you may be surprised to find that the longing for deep connection lives in all of us. Not everyone is conscious of this longing yet, but if you take the initiative and extend yourself, you likely will be touched by the beautiful responses you receive. And don't be surprised if the very act of asking someone to share this book with you awakens in that person a deep desire that he or she previously had not identified or admitted.

When thinking about an appropriate partner, choose someone with whom you already are in relationship, one which you feel has unrealized potentials. Ask yourself: *Does this relationship have the capacity for more openness? Could more unfold between us?* If the answer to these questions is "yes," then take a leap of faith and ask that person to read this book with you.

As mentioned before, the right person might not be your spouse or lover. If you contemplate the people in your life, you probably will know who to ask. If in doubt, consider this analogy: Most Ferraris sit in the garage, are rarely used, and hardly ever get the chance to reach their full capacity. Similarly, most relationships never realize their full potential due to the conventional way that most people connect. So think about who in your life has the capacity, energy, time and freedom to truly evolve.

Select a partner who shares your quest for
spiritual and emotional adventure,
a partner who is open to the potential
of creating an Evolutionary Relationship.

On the other hand, if you honestly cannot think of anyone with whom to explore mutual awakening, then please re-read the Prologue and Chapter One, and allow yourself to feel the longing for an Evolutionary Relationship. By keeping that longing alive, you will begin to attract people who are willing and ready to share a deeper connection. In the meantime, I encourage you to finish reading this book to prepare you for an Evolutionary Relationship when the appropriate person comes into your life.

Experiences of Mutual Awakening

I have taught mutual awakening to thousands of people all over the world, yet I find it an ever-new and always fascinating experience. The Mutual Awakening Practice is an exercise that you and your partner can return to again and again, and I will be inviting you to do it at the end of this chapter and as a warm-up exercise before some of the longer practices in this book. I love to hear what my students say about the Mutual Awakening Practice that is contained at the end of this chapter, especially if it is their first time doing the exercise. Here are a few descriptions from some of my students:

First I asked my partner, "What are you experiencing right now?" And I listened in rapt silence as she spoke for ten minutes in words that could have just as easily been my own. Her words resonated between us as "ours," holding the enormity, grit, and depth of humanity's stretch into something beyond itself — miraculously held, preciously and delicately between us.

~ Bernard, from Brooklyn, New York

When my turn to speak came, words poured out, adding another frame of down-to-earth details from a different life's perspective, adding to what we were together, building on it, going beyond and beyond again. The space in which we meet — what we are together — holds us in its power. The energy in the body is strong, the air shimmers, the space between us is alive and vibrant.

~ Alice, from Berkeley, California

In response to "What are we experiencing?" — we traded words, first from one then the other, hardly noticing who was speaking which phrase, adding to each other, building something together. I cannot fully explain what transpired, but I remember the awe!

~ Simon, from London, UK

The first time I engaged in the mutual awakening process, I sat across from someone I did not know, except for her first name. As we leaned into each other, I had the profound and profoundly simple experience of falling into love, of being pulled into the field of love that existed between us. All we had to do was be present and it revealed itself so strongly, so beautifully, beyond definition, pretense, and identity. One of the purest experiences of love in my life.

~ Vibeke, from Amsterdam, the Netherlands

While doing a mutual awakening practice, I began to describe my experience with emotions and how my physical body was feeling. Then the curiosity dropped deeper, and I began to describe qualities like openness, heavy areas, various colors blending, words like "melting bubbles" and "emerging oppositions" came out and I didn't know what I was talking about. But I was "seeing" it and intensely interested.

When I expanded my attention to include my partner, the "seeing" became brighter and somehow came closer. During the time when we shared what we were both experiencing, often we would say the same words, and we even discovered that we had the same taste in our mouths. I also noticed that sometimes silence would drop in so deeply that it took much effort to speak. It's a very mysterious process and it evoked a passionate yearning for me to feel deeper into my everyday experiences.

~ Ryan, from Dublin, Ireland

Practicing Together

Each chapter in this book contains practices and exercises, some of which are done on your own, either in silent contemplation or through journal writing. The most important practices, though, are those you will do with your partner, and the foundational exercise is the Mutual Awakening Practice which follows. Think of this practice as fundamental to mutual awakening in the same way that meditation is fundamental to individual awakening.

I recommend that you and your partner do the Mutual Awakening Practice at least once or twice a week for the first couple months, as you begin to explore this new inter-subjective terrain. Just remember to be patient — with yourself and with each other. This exercise will be your first deep dive into Evolutionary Relationships. It will require both of you staying open, deeply receptive, and simultaneously focused and attuned to yourself, each other, and the unfolding sense of the shared field. It will feel like you're learning a new dance. At first, you may feel awkward and step on each other's toes a bit. Midway through the book, you will start to feel more skillful and begin to dance in resonance. Eventually, if you continue to practice and use the Eight Activating Principles, you will know how it feels to "be danced" by something much greater than yourselves.

When you do an awakening practice with another person, I suggest that you approach the exercise with consciousness and care, just as you would if you were going to meditate by yourself. Create a safe space where you won't be disturbed, where you can relax and really be together. Before you begin each practice with your partner, close your eyes and spend two to ten minutes in silence. Let the momentum of the day slow down and let yourselves arrive in the moment together, ready to focus and fully available to each other.

Make sure both of you have taken time to read the relevant parts of the chapter, so that you have the context within which to do the practice. You also might take a few minutes and share with each other how you feel about entering into a particular practice together. Also, read the practice through first, so you feel clear about exactly how to do it and what to expect. Then begin.

Lastly, stay relaxed doing the exercises and venturing into this new domain of relatedness. It's new for all of us, so dismiss all worries about "doing it right." Simply follow the instructions and appreciate whatever happens, whatever emerges and evolves. And don't forget to appreciate yourself and your partner during the process. Thank you for accepting this invitation to experience mutual awakening.

EXERCISE:
Mutual Awakening Practice

The Mutual Awakening Practice is an exercise you do with a partner — whether a spouse, lover, friend, colleague, or even someone you've recently met — provided that person shares your interest in deepening the experience of mutuality. This practice is a portal to the profound dynamism of shared being. Like meditation, it is a simple practice but it requires focus, precision, and surrender to develop the capacity to enter into this space with reliability. So please be patient with yourself and your partner as you work with this practice.

It is best to be in the same room as your partner, but if this is not possible, you can adapt these instructions for use by video conference or telephone. The practice typically takes about 45 minutes, so make sure you have set aside enough time and will be free from distractions and interruptions.

Read through these instructions from beginning to end before you start the practice. You may prefer to use the audio download of these instructions, which is available at my website: www.EvolutionaryCollective.com.

Step 1: Connect with Yourself

Sit opposite your partner, preferably on chairs that are of equal height. You may want to set a timer for 5 minutes so that you don't need to watch the clock.

This first step is designed to help you connect with your authentic self by feeling an intimacy and closeness with yourself and your experience. Close your eyes and invite yourself to arrive and be fully present. Give attention to your body and open up your consciousness to include whatever physical sensations you are feeling. Don't narrow your focus, but rather be open to the totality of what is present in your body. Note the particular sensations that come into your awareness.

Next, turn your attention to your heart and emotions, opening up another channel of awareness and closeness with yourself, while retaining consciousness of your body. Notice if there are any strong reactions or subtle effects or moods present.

(continued on next page)

Lastly, include your mind. Focus on the sensation and movement of thoughts through your awareness, rather than their content. Notice if there is a sense of fogginess and confusion, or lightness and clarity. Observe whether your mind is active and agitated or quiet and still.

Take a deep breath and accept and include all of the experience that is present — in your body, your heart, and your mind. Now open your eyes.

Step 2: Connect with Each Other

The second step is about connecting with your partner. As you open your eyes, allow yourself to include the other person in your awareness, just as you opened to include the various levels of your own experience. Simply allow yourself to be present, experiencing whatever you might be apprehending as you allow your partner to be there with you. Look into each other's eyes as you do this.

After about a minute, ask yourself: *Am I the right distance from my partner for the optimum connection?* Don't think about this with your mind; listen for what intuitively feels right. Experiment together, moving closer and farther away, until you discover a distance where the connection is easy to find and feel. It may feel a little uncomfortable or too intimate, but be courageous in discovering the position that allows you to feel the connection. I recommend that you err on the side of "too close."

Next, set a timer for 5 minutes. Once you are settled, simply look into each other's eyes and allow the other to exist in your field of awareness and relatedness. There is nothing to do, no special experience that should or shouldn't be happening, just an allowing and including of yourself and the other.

Step 3: What Are You Experiencing?

This step allows each of you to focus deeply and completely on the other. Set a timer for 10 minutes and decide which of you will go first. If you are starting, then your partner will ask you the question: *What are you experiencing right now?*

Be open, transparent, and intimate with whatever is arising in your experience and share it as directly as you can. Describe the experience with textures, temperature, color, structures, shapes, images, and feelings, rather than concepts. For example, a concept might be, "I feel agitated," but the direct experience would be, "There's a shakiness, a very slight vibration through my lower belly. I can feel a hint of sadness, an achiness moving through the left side of my body. Now there's a light in the distance that I'm aware of ..." and so on.

Release yourself from the need to "make sense" or entertain your partner. Whatever you are experiencing, just follow it, staying close to where your experience is originating. If something shifts mid-sentence, that's fine. Let it lead you where it wants to go. If you feel nothing, ask yourself: *Exactly what is the "nothing" I am present to?*

If from time to time you want to close your eyes in order to focus on something that is arising, feel free to do that, but then open your eyes again to share the experience with your partner. Don't edit or censor your perceptions — stay open, curious, and vulnerable. Follow anything that you feel pulled to explore more deeply. You're not trying to get anywhere or solve a problem. Your goal is to simply stay close to what is arising and articulate it to your partner as directly as possible.

When the 10 minutes is up, set the timer again and switch roles. Ask your partner: *What are you experiencing right now?* Now your job is to focus as deeply and completely on your partner as you can. You want to be so close in your active listening that you feel your partner's experience as they express it. If it feels right, from time to time you can ask the question freshly for them to answer.

You will find that if you truly stay close to your partner and their immediate experience, your own thoughts will disappear. Conversely, if you have the conscious command to think about what they are saying or to judge them, you aren't focused closely enough.

Ideally, this practice gives you 10 minutes to completely let go of your normal identification with your own interior space and to focus completely on the other person to the point where you begin to actualize their experience as your own. Initially, you may not be able to empathize at this deep level nor to hold that space for the full ten minutes. But keep trying. Let go of yourself, give your energy to your partner, and see what can happen.

(continued on next page)

Step 4: What Are We Experiencing?

The final step is to focus on the space between you both. Set the timer for 10 minutes, and this time ask the question: *What are we experiencing right now?*

In order to answer this question, both of you will need to place your attention on the space between you — the place where your consciousness overlaps. Rather than going one at a time, take short turns answering the question, looping back and forth between you.

As you go back and forth, try not to answer with your mind, but rather let yourself speak from the space of the connection — the we-space. The question is not: *What do you think we are experiencing?* The point of the exercise to access what the we-space has to say. A good way to keep this exercise on track is to start your answer with: *We are experiencing ...* This may feel a little strange at first, but within a few minutes, you will discover a flow together.

At the end of the 10 minutes, thank your partner. The practice is now over. If you have the time, close your eyes and notice the influence that the practice has had on you. Feel into your own experience and notice where you are now. Does it feel different than where you were at the beginning of the practice? Each partner also might like to share how this first exercise on mutual awakening felt. ✂

For supplementary content, including audios, videos, and exercises, visit: www.EvolutionaryRelationshipsBook.com/bonus

Notes

1   Sufi Path of Love, http://sufipathoflove.com/sufism.

2   Olga Louchakova, "The Experience of Sohbet," International Association of Sufism, http://www.ias.org/spf/sohbet.html.

PART II
EVOLUTIONARY
RELATIONSHIPS
Introduction: The Eight Activating Principles

In working with thousands of people to develop the experience and expression of evolutionary mutuality, I've identified "Eight Activating Principles," which I'll be sharing in the chapters that follow. These principles will allow you to recognize and create evolutionary mutuality and then to develop, sustain, and deepen it.

The Activating Principles act as catalysts. They trigger and ignite a new form of relatedness. They also provide an energetic quality that the relationship will continue to express in a naturally evolving form. With each of these Activating Principles, I encourage you first to read through the chapter fully, in order to get an overall understanding of what I mean, and then try some of the exercises and contemplations, either alone or with a partner. As you enter into an Evolutionary Relationship, return to these principles to make adjustments and align the relationship so that it is more and more congruent with these elements. The Activating Principles are not linear steps, but more like a series of dials on an amplifier — they need to be tuned and balanced so that the potentials of your relationship are amplified and eventually resonate with these new qualities.

The Activating Principles offer various ways to orient yourself as you are relating, so that your relationship is catalyzed into its higher potentials. Each element contributes to the flavor of what is shaping and empowering the relationship. As you grow personally and your relationship matures and deepens, you will discover how to naturally and effortlessly "turn up the volume" on each of these principles. Then, as these principles are turned up, you will be able to work through whatever is obstructing your capacity to fully embrace them, and your relationships will come alive. The evolutionary impulse will accelerate your relationship, by deconstructing and dissolving membranes of separation and by shedding inauthentic and disingenuous methods of relating.

Eventually, the intensity of the relatedness will shift your sense of self beyond egoic patterns and something greater will take over. The optimizing force will move through you and between you and your partner with ever-greater power as the inertia of both your egos dissipates. The more deeply you both surrender to the potential of your connection, the more passionately engaged, committed, attuned to the truth, and trusting you will be together. You will feel support from a larger and more magnificent force than either of you could generate on your own. The power of being related will organically move you into higher and higher dimensions of awakening, creativity, and love.

Here is a summary of the Eight Activating Principles of evolutionary mutuality, which we will explore in depth in this section of the book:

1. **Engagement:** Wholehearted engagement and genuine interest in what happens within the relationship. Saying "yes" to being fully connected.

2. **Commitment:** Mutual commitment to each other and to the relationship, expressed as a willingness to "stay on the inside" even if something is not working, instead of taking oneself out of the relationship.

3. **Truth:** A shared love of truth and transparency, and a desire to explore reality together — a journey which will lead to deeper intimacy with oneself, each other, and life.

4. **Trust:** The ability to generate trust together (even while knowing that we inevitably will disappoint each other), and a willingness to allow this field of mutual trust to restore a more universal trust in life itself.

5. **Openness:** A presence and availability for whatever arises in the moment, which allows the field of the relationship to offer all of its possibilities.

6. **Essential Uniqueness:** A distinct dimension of identity that allows this new potential of relatedness to flower. Authentic essential autonomy is developed and strengthened inside the sacred communion of the relationship.

7. **Contact:** A deep respect for each person's essential, unique being that touches each person's soul outside the boundaries of the personality.

8. **Mutual Influence:** The desire to positively affect each other and to develop an Evolutionary Relationship. This sacred intent creates a field of sensitivity and responsibility that allows the relationship to thrive on multiple levels and dimensions.

CHAPTER FOUR
The First Principle: Engagement

I have come to drag you out of yourself, and take you in my heart.
I have come to bring out the beauty you never knew you had
and lift you like a prayer to the sky.

~ Rumi

One of the simplest but most powerful words in the English language is "YES!" It is the heart of "engagement" — the First Activating Principle of Evolutionary Relationships.

Mutuality depends on each person actively engaging in the relationship and saying "yes" to being connected. Conversely, when we identify with ego, we become accustomed to functioning in a state of withholding — holding back our real feelings, our energy, our intimate thoughts and experiences. We resist real contact. Of course, there's value in having developed the maturity to self-regulate our expression and be sensitive to each other's privacy. But to create mutuality, we need to stop withholding and subtly (or not-so-subtly) saying "no" to each other.

"Yes" is more than a word that gives permission. It's an expression of the creative universal force of life, a force that strives toward union, love, and evolution. Saying "yes" is a way of personally accessing the evolutionary impulse; it is an openness that allows us to expand and initiate giving and receiving fully.

An Evolutionary Relationship is by definition mutual — it requires two or more people to say "yes" and consciously choose to accept one another and engage together. Sometimes you feel drawn toward a friend, lover, or colleague, but for one reason or another you never really commit to actualizing what's possible between you. Perhaps you feel a "yes" but for some reason they express "no."

For example, I have a friend I've known for many years — a beautiful, powerful woman, who is innovative in her field. We have complementary skills and a true love for each other. At one point we began a conversation about working together but it never went anywhere because she relished her independence. I felt the potential of what we might have created together and how we might have been transformed by each other, but without an understanding of mutuality, nothing could happen. If you've had a similar experience, don't be discouraged. The percentage of people who are ready to create Evolutionary Relationships is still relatively small, but it is growing. And the more of us who learn how to do it, the easier it will be for other people to discover as we move into the future.

An Invitation to Mutual Engagement

This first principle, engagement, is crucial if there is to be evolutionary mutuality. Engagement means we invite each other to be fully open to what is occurring between us in the moment. Even such a simple invitation has unexpected power. Being invited to really show up creates a transformative portal which activates the possibilities between us. For the most part, however, we live in a world where we almost never are invited to give fully of ourselves or share our gifts completely. Consequently, being engaged means being present and authentically putting ourselves on the line in order to be in relationship with someone else.

If we honestly examine our normal way of relating, what we'll discover is that many of our relationships exist largely in our imagination — in projections, images, fantasies, and ideas of who we are, who the other person is, and what our relationship represents. Either we are unaware that anything more is possible, or we're too afraid to penetrate the veil of the "real" and find out what actually exists between us. So typically we don't show up fully because we're reluctant to face what we may encounter within ourselves, our partner, and the relationship.

Often with conventional relationships, we're just seeking stability, familiarity, or a situation we don't have to worry about, much like owning a reliable car that runs well and doesn't require much maintenance. In such cases, we want our relationships to be enjoyable and supportive, but we don't want to exert too much effort or take too many risks. There's nothing wrong with such basic needs, as we all require support and stability in our lives. However, if that's where our desires stop, the full potential of our relationships will never be activated. There is no true engagement in such relationships. They may be comfortable and safe, but they are not satisfying because no essential nourishment occurs and nothing is being exchanged at a soul level.

Relationships like this have no zeal, since engagement is what activates the dynamism between two people. Imagine two dancers who are not really engaged: They shuffle halfheartedly around the floor, out of time with each other and the music. Now imagine those same dancers fully engaged with each other and the dance: Their every step bursts with vitality and is perfectly synchronized with the rhythm of the music.

We all know what it feels like when someone is with us but not really engaged. Remember when you were a kid and you tried to tell your mom a story that was really important to you about what happened in school that day? You could tell she was only half listening, with the other half of her attention focused on preparing dinner. I'm sure you've also had the experience of trying to converse with someone who is more engaged with his or her cell phone than with you.

A while back, I was dating a man who was leaving for work and who kissed me goodbye in a way that felt unconscious. It was a throwaway kiss — he already was partly out the door and not present with me or the kiss. I smiled and said, "What was that supposed to be?" He turned around, walked toward me, then *really* kissed me. He engaged fully; I felt him and I felt us. By asking that question, I invited him to engage and he did. How many moments in your life are like that? How often do you accept superficial contact? For many of us, we've become accustomed to living with a level of unconsciousness that maintains separation.

In Evolutionary Relationships,
partners help each other stay open,
connected, available, and motivated.
Unconscious words and superficial behaviors
are not part of the engagement repertoire.

Most people accept disengagement and unconsciousness without question. We rarely demand of ourselves or each other that we show up fully and offer ourselves to the moment. A disconnected coexistence feels "normal" to most people and, sadly, is oftentimes preferable.

In the future, say twenty or thirty years from now, I believe we humans will have evolved our ability to relate. Perhaps we'll look back on today's conventional relationships the way we now look back at racial segregation — as a social pattern that once felt normal but now seems bizarre, crude, and hard to comprehend. I also predict that in the future we'll understand that maintaining separation was the source of many of the world's problems — problems that true relatedness can begin to solve today.

Showing Up As Your Essential Self

In order to fully engage in the manner I've been describing, we have to be willing to show up as our essential self. As we discussed in the previous chapter, our ego-selves are defined by our boundaries and sense of separation. When we inhabit our egos, we cannot experience mutuality. Most of us identify with our egos as a coping mechanism when we come into contact with others.

We unconsciously project personas, such as: the brash, charismatic, confident leader; the tough, no-nonsense person who's got it all figured out; the shy, retiring outsider; the deep, sensitive spiritual person; the helpful, attentive friend.

These habitual personas are not who we are at the core level. Nevertheless, we tend to use these personas to interact in the world, while our essential self remains hidden. To truly engage means to let the essential self come forward with honesty and candor. Showing up in this way does not mean we bare our soul to just anyone or that we make our self emotionally vulnerable. Rather, engaging requires stepping into the field of relatedness with another person and being open, authentic, and dropping our defenses in a way that is appropriate to the moment.

Right now for a few moments, close your eyes and sense into that part of you that represents your core being, a place often associated with the deeper center of your heart. If you are unsure where the seat of your soul lives, it's the part of you that comes alive when you feel deeply loved, as when you've let your lover in or held your baby for the first time. It's a place where you allow others to see who you really are.

Often, we are shy about showing how much beauty, goodness, or power we possess because we've gotten used to sharing the more superficial layers of ourselves. But there is a deeper, vaster self we can reveal if we wish. In the past fifty years or so, as culture has become more sensitive to the depths of the individual self, some of us have been brave enough to share our woundedness with friends, to reveal our shadow sides with therapists, and to unveil our weaknesses to healers. As a result, many of us now are ready to reveal our core self, our authentic self, the self who transcends our personas, our stories, and our wounds.

It can feel risky to express who we really are, to let ourselves touch and be touched by the world, to affect and be affected by others. It takes courage to let ourselves be unveiled and visible. As tribal animals, we instinctively fear rejection and ostracism. In fact, scientists have discovered that social rejection activates the same regions in our brain as physical pain. Once upon a time, our very survival depended on being accepted by our clan, and although times have changed, we are hard-wired to play it safe by conforming to societal norms. The stakes are even higher if we are rejected after exposing our essence and engaging with other people on a deep level, which is why we tend to hold back and insulate our core self.

In extreme cases, a person may withdraw from other people and the world, or present a completely inauthentic self, keeping their deeper self fully hidden. The risks associated with exposing our deeper self are not imaginary, especially if we've historically been hurt, betrayed, rejected, or abandoned. Indeed, if others have abused or taken advantage of us, it's completely understandable that we may hesitate to come out.

Moreover, even when we bravely and fully show up, we assume the risk of our vulnerability not being reciprocated, our authenticity not being appreciated. We also open ourselves to disappointment, especially when we allow our expectations to rise by embracing the possibility that something extraordinary might happen. Some people are equally afraid of sublime and exquisite experiences as they are of the darkness and shadows. In sum, many of us have learned the hard way that showing up and exposing ourselves can be dangerous. Out of fear of upsetting others, provoking anger or disapproval, or disrupting the status quo, we tone ourselves down, hold back our fullness, dampen our beauty, mute our magnificence.

If we want to experience the higher potentials of relatedness, these are risks we must be willing to take. There always will be people who misunderstand true engagement, who simply don't get it. That's why courage is an essential ingredient for this First Activating Principle. Just remember: Engagement is mutual, so you need to find another soul who is willing to fully engage.

The Courage to Engage

No one would question that relationships are an adventure. It takes courage to bring out the aliveness, the potentials that exist between us. Some people climb mountains, fight battles and risk their physical safety for adventure, but they're afraid to expose their hearts to another human being. Without courage and the willingness to take risks together, a relationship cannot thrive.

Courage can be viewed not only as a momentary act but as a level of consciousness — a way of orienting oneself toward life. People approach life from different fundamental perspectives that flavor and filter their way of functioning. Dr. David Hawkins, in his book *Transcending the Levels of Consciousness*, describes courage as a consciousness level that is energetically positive and generative, and which allows for real mutuality and reciprocity. "Courage is the first true level of power," he writes. "Only at the level of courage do we put back into the world as much energy as we take from it."[1]

When we function from a less courageous, more fearful level of consciousness, we tend to be locked into survival and self-absorption, and we therefore are unable to really connect with others. Moreover, at lower levels of consciousness, we are more apt to lie and deceive ourselves and others in order to protect ourselves and get what we want. A lack of interest and engagement is another reflection of a lower state of consciousness, one that is fearful and reticent. If your heart is present only when things feel safe and secure, you are not being courageous.

When we have courage, however, we are willing to be authentic, even if it means that we risk losing something or someone or our self-image is challenged. Courage also implies the willingness to be open and try new things. It enables us to take risks and explore what is possible. This type of bravery evokes a sense of adventure, curiosity and excitement, rather than fear in the face of the unknown. Even if there is fear, when we come from the consciousness of courage, we say "yes" and engage anyway. The courageous heart is a heart that is present and open, regardless of what may happen. In this way, courage gives us the positive energy, resilience, and flexibility to stay related and fully involved so we can learn and grow together.

When we recognize true courage in another person, it touches us at a soul level. I think that's the main reason many people love television shows like *Survivor* and *America's Got Talent*. Yes, some viewers watch these shows just to see people fail or make fools of themselves during the early auditions. But most people watch for those moments when some unlikely character, nervous and awkward, meets a difficult physical challenge or steps onto the stage to sing and blows everyone away with the unexpected beauty of true talent.

Deep displays of vulnerability touch us and a willingness to take risks inspires us. There is a rawness to such authenticity — a palpable sense of courage that keeps us riveted, alert, and vicariously proud of the other person's accomplishment. During the process of watching others exhibit bravery, we discover new dimensions of ourselves. And when we are mutually engaged with a partner who demonstrates courage, we simultaneously are activated by the brave dynamic between us, which then frees the evolutionary impulse to take us even further.

Practicing Engagement

If you've worked on your own spiritual awakening, you've learned how to bring awareness to different dimensions of yourself. You've also realized that unless you reach a deep level of self-inquiry, you are essentially asleep and moving through life unconsciously. The same principle applies to our relationships. We no longer should relate to others unconsciously or be disengaged. In order to "wake up the relationship" we need to pay attention to the field between us and determine what we can do to engage more fully.

Now is the time to start paying attention to the level of engagement in your close relationships. If you have a partner who is willing and interested, a great way to begin is to practice simply reflecting back to each other those moments when you "lose" each other. First, establish why each of you is interested in the relationship. Then ask: *What can I do to engage more fully?* Choose a certain period of time, an evening for example, when you agree to be fully present together and interested in whatever is occurring between you. Notice what creates separation. It might be a sense of distance suddenly appearing, a recognition that the other person seems distracted or closed, or just a feeling that "something changed." Draw attention to those moments without trying yet to fix them. Simply become aware that you've disengaged or checked-out and then bring yourselves back to full engagement and presence.

Peter and I instinctively sought to maintain closeness even while doing mundane tasks. For example, I remember a day when we left our apartment on West Fifty-Sixth Street in New York City to go grocery shopping. We took turns putting items in our shopping cart, occasionally kissing and feeling very light and connected. We got to the checkout, and I felt Peter's energy dissipate just slightly — I experienced it as a contraction in the space between us. When we left the store I asked him what had happened. He admitted noticing an attractive woman in front of me who was dressed elegantly in European fashion, and he had started to judge me because I dressed like an American. He said these thoughts made him feel guilty, so he withdrew just a little. I laughed and said, "Yes, I do dress like an American!" Immediately, we were fully engaged again, and the space between us opened back up. The secret to true intimacy is deceptively simple: Just pay attention to whatever comes between you and your partner.

> *Ironically, true engagement often starts when partners recognize its absence. By acknowledging distractions and moments of separation, we bear witness to a lack of intimacy which we'll want to restore.*

On another occasion, Peter was sleeping late while I had been awake for hours, buzzing around our apartment and getting chores done. I finally came to the bedroom to wake him with a cup of tea, and as he sat up in bed and took the tea from my hand, he said in his soft German accent, "Where's my woman?" I thought he was joking, and I replied, "I'm right here." He said it again, with more seriousness, and I couldn't figure out what he was asking me. So I answered again, "I am right here," and he repeated his question for the third time, but this time he looked deeply into my eyes and pulled me onto the bed in a powerful embrace. I then realized he was asking for my full presence, and the intensity of his gesture melted me. He said softly, "Oh … there you are!" We kissed and then moved into a deeper state of consciousness and connection than we had ever shared before.

Looking back on such precious moments with Peter brings tears to my eyes, not just because we were in love, but because we were so fully, completely engaged with one another on a soul level. Today, I understand that what we shared was an ongoing commitment to being fully present with each other, staying engaged no matter what arose, and never allowing each other to withdraw or disconnect without a direct challenge to restore the intimacy. By loving and being with each other in this way, Peter and I became one, and we lived from a oneness that was immeasurably valuable.

As human beings, we have the potential to discover and enjoy an embodied "oneness" with another person. But first, we have to be willing to reach beyond ourselves into the consciousness of unity. This is a practice you can do only in a relationship where you and your partner are equally interested in exploring the higher domains of love and have given each other permission to point out when intimacy has broken down or diminished.

A Love that Demands Further Engagement

Often when we think of love, what comes to mind is acceptance, caring, sweetness, warmth, forgiveness, generosity, and kindness. Many of the great spiritual teachers have taught us the value of unconditional love — a love that doesn't ask anything from others. But there is another dimension to love that is exquisitely demanding, unquenchable in its desire for you to give all of who you are. This type of love requires your totality, your full presence, and everything you possibly can give in the moment ... and then some. This kind of love draws forth your depths and calls you to engage with it fully. The force of this love is connected to infinite and divine possibilities, as it encapsulates the potential of the universe.

In addition, this particular love is innately selfless — it beckons you to allow the other person to be who they truly are, rather than the person you might want them to be or a person with something to give you. This love sees and knows that each of us is infinite and that each of us has the right to fulfill our highest potential. To be wholeheartedly loved in this way is truly life changing. Many people fail to achieve this dimension of love because they are afraid that the unhealed aspects of their nature — immaturity, addiction, poor self-esteem, etc. — will permit their defensive or demanding ego-self to take over. Yet it's worth taking the risk of healing your wounds, since when they arise they prevent the full power of love from coming through you.

Sadly, most of us don't allow ourselves to care that much about people who are outside our immediate circle of family and friends. Even with close relations, we tend to place expectations on each other, stemming from a place of egoic judgment or personal agenda. And sometimes we merely tolerate each other and are careful not to ask for too much, lest we feel the need to reciprocate.

The bottom line is that it's good to feel loved, accepted, and supported just as we are. Indeed, this is the most important dimension of love, and we need to learn how to love each other unconditionally if we wish to fulfill our higher potentials. It is essential to recognize and include this demanding dimension of love if we are to access and grow though its power.

Not surprisingly, child development psychologists have confirmed the importance of both forms of love I've been describing. It is now well known that children need what influential 20th Century psychologist Donald Winnicott calls a "holding environment" — a safe, accepting, and loving environment in which children's basic needs are met and they feel nurtured, protected, understood, loved and supported. What is less widely understood is that children also need an adult figure in their lives, often their mother, who recognizes and mirrors their unique nature, sees their potential, and supports them to fully realize that potential. The same holds true throughout our development: Everyone needs to be supported and to have their potentials acknowledged and called forth.

I've only met a few people in my life who generously opened this demanding channel of love toward me, and those are the relationships that have permanently molded and imprinted my life. When you truly are loved unconditionally, you experience the passion of being invited to be your highest and best self. Through that special parent, mentor, or friend, you learn that the universe cares you are here. In fact, the universe *demands* that you give yourself fully to your own life and to the lives of others, because it matters. Here's an analogy: Imagine you're a singer, standing backstage after a performance, and you hear the audience clapping and stomping for more. Eventually, you're compelled to return to the stage, even though you don't yet know which song you will sing as an encore.

At the age of eighteen when I met my first mentor Werner Erhard, he saw and demanded my full potential (and everyone else's) in a way that allowed me to discover my true self as a teacher. Later, this role was taken on by Peter, who unceasingly and relentlessly called forth depths of beauty and love I didn't even know I could access, much less embody. Peter made me feel like I was coming in contact with the heart of God, a force that wants us to have everything, but only if we open ourselves to our highest potential.

This heightened state of mutual engagement activates an extraordinary level of generosity and abundance. There exists an invisible realm of relationships associated with the flow of giving and receiving. Relationships thrive on equilibrium, made up of give-and-take actions that service and sustain them. For instance, if we do something that endangers or damages a relationship, we feel guilt. Similarly, we will feel shame if the giving and receiving are not balanced. Conversely, we feel free and pure when our actions serve the relationship, as when we receive fully and then give a little more in return. Generosity of spirit activates an upward flow, consistent with the optimizing force of the cosmos.

Some people fall into an over-giving, martyr mode when they help others and deny their own needs. The danger here is that they eventually will feel resentful and entitled, which creates a hostile environment for intimacy and relatedness. In extreme cases, such people minimize what they need from life and from others, thereby closing themselves off to the point of not wanting to take anything. The person who gives without taking from another is positioning him or herself to be either superior and separate or codependent and isolated. Their involvement in the relationship is limited and shallow, and it doesn't invite a deep engagement or exchange.

Full exchange is at the heart of all Evolutionary Relationships. Mutuality means that we are committed to giving and receiving equally and to the fullest extent of our capacity.

Peter and I used to say we felt like millionaires because we knew we were living in the extraordinary richness of our deep love and the way in which we fully gave to and received from each other. Interestingly, when we were together, neither Peter nor I had access to a lot of money, but we lived in abundance. We were given jobs that we loved and worked only two days a week. The rest of the time we spent together. We traveled in Europe and were given places to live: a millionaire's apartment in Berlin, a villa in Italy, a private beach house in East Hampton with a pool and tennis court, and so forth. It is amazing how well the universe supported us. I believe we were graced with beauty and abundance in direct proportion to the level of pure exchange between us.

EXERCISE:
Practicing Engagement

Allow at least 30 to 45 minutes to explore the power of engagement with your partner. Start by sitting across from each other on chairs, with your knees touching or almost touching.

Step 1. Close your eyes and allow yourself to settle into the moment, inviting yourself to be fully present. Gather all of yourself and let the motion and momentum of the day slowly come to a stop. Give yourselves 5 to 10 minutes to fully arrive.

Step 2. Open your eyes and allow yourself to look into the eyes of your partner. There is nothing particular to do; just allow yourselves to share the space and experience of being with each other.

Step 3. Next, decide who will speak first and who will be the listener. Before the speaker begins, spend a few moments feeling into the deepest part of your self — the part that is rarely seen, shared, or given. See if you can get in touch with your core self, and as you do, prepare to speak from that core.

As the speaker prepares, the listener should prepare to be attentive, open, and sensitive. Be ready to listen from "inside" the speaker and stay inside as he or she shares. Let go of thinking, reflecting, judging, or interpreting what the speaker will say, and definitely don't worry about preparing a response. Simply allow yourself to get lost in the speaker, to become one with him or her.

(continued on next page)

Step 4. Now, each of you will have 10 minutes to speak. The speaker should start by sharing the experience of his or her inner core — what I call the "origination point" — the deepest place where we came into this world as unique.

- ⌘ What would it feel like to have your partner truly see and accept your depth?
- ⌘ What would it feel like to have your partner support the fullness of who you are?
- ⌘ What could be created if you were challenged by your partner to be even more than you are now, to move beyond your perceived limited resources?
- ⌘ What potentials and possibilities might come into existence with that type of support and encouragement?

Explore the possibilities. Also explore how a more demanding sort of love would work or not work for you. Then, ask your partner if he or she truly wants to support the fullness of who you are. After the first speaker finishes, switch roles and have your partner share how it would feel for him or her to be fully supported and wanted.

Step 5. Switch roles again for a 5 minute round. This time, share your fears and concerns. Then have your partner do the same.

Step 6. Now, both of you close your eyes and get in touch with the benevolent force that invites your true self to come forth, that wants everything that is possible for you, and that offers all the support you could possibly need. Then have your partner do the same.

Step 7. Lastly, discuss if you are willing to commit to one another — *even though you're not sure what that means yet* — in order to discover how to love each other in a way that deeply challenges and totally supports both of you as individuals and the evolving Evolutionary Relationship.

(continued on next page)

Step 8. If you both are willing to support each other, craft a commitment and say it out loud to each other. Plan to work together again in a few days or within the next week. ☙

For supplementary content, including audios, videos, and exercises, visit: www.EvolutionaryRelationshipsBook.com/bonus

Notes

1   David R. Hawkins, *Transcending the Levels of Consciousness: The Stairway to Enlightenment*, West Sedona, AZ: Veritas Publishing, 2006.

CHAPTER FIVE
The Second Principle: Commitment

The moment one definitely commits oneself, then
Providence moves too … raising in one's favour all manner
of unforeseen incidents and meetings and material assistance,
which no man could have dreamt would have come his way.

~ William H. Murray

Commitment is the second of the Eight Activating Principles. The first principle, engagement, begins the relationship and sets in motion the powerful experience of mutuality and dynamic intimacy. Driven by courage and curiosity, we take a leap into a new dimension of relatedness. But if we are to sustain this unfamiliar level of intense connectedness, with the opportunities for love and creativity that it provides, it's going to take more than engagement.

We've all heard of the "honeymoon phase" in romantic relationships, and we know what tends to happen once it's over. Things get more challenging. The same principle applies in any relationship that has the power and potential of an Evolutionary Relationship. Initially, we experience openings and synergies that inspire us, but inevitably unforeseen interpersonal dynamics bring forth the necessary challenges that will enable us to continue growing and developing. When staying connected gets harder, one or both partners will "drop out" and somehow justify not staying with the process and the connection. That's where commitment comes in. Mutual commitment anchors us in the relationship no matter what challenges may arise.

Redefining Commitment

Many of us hear the word "commitment" and have an instinctive reaction of resistance. We're often reluctant to commit ourselves, yet we readily judge others for their lack of commitment. It's a word that comes loaded with cultural associations, many of which are negative. For some of us, it raises the specter of our parents' or grandparents' old-fashioned and often religious ideas about commitment, such as the notion that we should stay married to the same person no matter what and "till death do us part." We're all familiar with how suffocating that level of unquestioning commitment can be. Back in the 1950s, if you committed to a marriage, a career path, or a traditional role, you implicitly were agreeing to limited life choices. For women, a terrific book on this topic is the 1964 classic *The Feminine Mystique* by Betty Friedan, which still is applicable for some cultural pockets of the world.

As popular culture evolved, however, the feminist and civil rights revolutions of the 1960s and 1970s shattered many traditional roles and the commitments that went with them. A new individualism emerged, and postmodern memes began to supersede the earlier cultural bonds, resulting in the attitude that we would stay committed to each other only so long as we were getting what we want from each other and from the relationship. Consequently, if a relationship helped us fulfill our goals, we would stay committed. However, the moment one partner felt they were no longer getting what they wanted out of the relationship, they were free to opt out.

In this next stage of cultural development, personal happiness and personal fulfillment became paramount in relationships. For many of us, our primary commitment became a pledge of personal power to ourselves.

For example, staying in marriages that made us miserable no longer made sense, nor did sticking to a chosen career path when it was unfulfilling. We embraced our freedom, throwing off the shackles of commitments that held us down and limited our individual potential.

These cultural changes played a critical role in redefining societal norms. Specifically, many people benefited from an increase in personal freedom and an attunement to individuality, which fostered inner growth and development. We struggled to become more sensitized to our own needs and our unique paths, but I believe we may have gone too far. Consider the rising divorce rates, the non-committal dating habits of Millennials, and the extreme polarization between "conservative" and "liberal" worldviews. Many of us seem to have lost the capacity to be deeply committed to each other and to something bigger than ourselves. We fail to recognize that there are goals worth sacrificing for and difficulties worth living through in order to manifest our collective higher potential. Too often, we bail out on relationships the moment challenges arise. The closest we come to commitment is a willingness to "do the best we can."

In our postmodern culture, we've lowered social standards and often dwell on our woundedness rather than our actual potential. It's time to embrace a bigger vision for ourselves and our community that includes our hard-won self-awareness but also reaches beyond its limitations.

The postmodern era has resulted in a preoccupation with the growth of self over the progress of society. By cultivating Evolutionary Relationships, we enter a field of mutual introspection that benefits us all.

We've all suffered the consequences of this resistance to commitment. How many times have you met someone with whom you felt a deep connection — a chemistry that was inspiring and real and begged to be further explored — but then never heard from that person again because there was no particular commitment to what was discovered or to the potentials that were beginning to emerge? Sadly, we've become accustomed to a kind of "social promiscuity" — not necessarily in our sexual adventures but in other areas of life. We justify not being committed by telling ourselves we're "going with the flow" or "following our bliss" or "being in the moment" and "listening to our guidance." While it is important to be open to change and to follow our intuition regarding where our destiny lies, we also need to listen to something greater than ourselves, which requires a new kind of commitment.

We need to take responsibility, if in one moment mutual engagement presents itself but then it elusively dissipates. It's disheartening and exhausting when we keep letting each other down due to our unwillingness to commit and build something sacred in our relationships. It's easy to become bitter and cynical. I have had to recover from such dead-end interactions, and I've found that it takes real work to continue being open, loving, and willing to engage in a culture where commitment is withheld. This is not an individual problem; it's a cultural malaise that each of us has to struggle with in order to grow together.

In order to commit, I'm not suggesting we go back to the kind of rigid and limiting commitments of our grandparents' era. Rather, I am suggesting that we expand ourselves to include much more than just our personal desires so that we can access a higher sense of guidance as we navigate our relationships. As we wake up to the truth of our interconnectedness with each other and with all life, our commitments should reflect this heightened awareness. We must integrate how much we impact each other and the potential that we can bring forth through our mutual commitment. Only then will our commitments reflect the greater context in which we live, love, and collectively flourish.

What Are We Committed To?

When we enter into the domain of evolutionary mutuality, commitment becomes more than just a blind loyalty to our self or to our partner. We remain committed to our own development and the fulfillment of our individual destiny, but we are equally committed to the development of our partner and the fulfillment of his or her destiny as well. In sum, we commit to the potential of the relationship itself, to mutual awakening, and to listening to larger forces with which we come into contact through an opening we create together. This kind of mutual commitment does not preserve the *status quo*. Instead, it enables us to pursue what's possible and let go of what is no longer serving that potential — no matter where this new path may lead us. It's a commitment that aligns us with the greater design, allowing us to attune to the dynamism of the evolutionary impulse which has the power to move both partners forward.

As you enter into a committed Evolutionary Relationship, it is essential to be very conscious and explicit about what you are actually committing to do together. Without awareness, there can be unconscious commitments that have not been made explicit and may drive our behaviors without us even realizing it.

In an Evolutionary Relationship, commitment is even more critical than in a conventional relationship, because the stakes are higher. An Evolutionary Relationship is not just about creating stability; it's about bringing forth new potentials and creating genuine breakthroughs in what's possible for you *and* for humanity. There are certain potentials that will not come into existence without this mutual dimension of consciousness — potentials that affect those around us as well.

When I worked with my first teacher Werner Erhard, he created a technology around what it takes to create breakthroughs. In this context, I am defining a "breakthrough" as something you sincerely want but don't know how to create. A breakthrough is unpredictable, not something you can achieve with linear thinking, planning, or control. Instead, the path of creating a breakthrough emerges through your longing for and commitment to something beyond what you think is possible. So each time there is a breakdown — something that doesn't work or some pattern within you or the situation that is insufficient to support a new potential — you have the opportunity to see what is missing and discover new pathways. Additionally, when a system or situation breaks down or falls apart, a new opening is created that may allow you to let go of old identities, habits, and ways of being.

Innovation is rarely comfortable or easy. Therefore, it is essential that you be committed if you wish to muster the strength to handle breakdowns and breakthroughs. The key is to courageously use the obstacles that present themselves as opportunities for growth.

When we commit to an Evolutionary Relationship, we act as pioneers for the greater good of humanity, bravely paving the way for those who follow in our footsteps.

Another source of strength comes from the knowledge that the powerful potentials of your Evolutionary Relationship may reveal breakthroughs not only for you and your partner, but also for how human beings can deeply connect with each other in general. Your shared process sets a beautiful example of what any human being must deal with in order to let go of conventional habits of separation. As you and your partner develop the ability to hold intense levels of love and creativity and become comfortable with these new abilities and sensitivities, the potential for breakthroughs becomes more accessible for all.

Creating New Cultural Habits

When we venture into the higher potentials of relatedness with another human being, we begin to realize new possibilities for humanity as a whole, and we create new patterns of being and relating that others will be inspired to follow. The deeper our commitment, the more stable these new patterns will become.

Social scientists and psychologists sometimes describe our cultural tendencies and customs as habits — not just personal habits but cultural habits. For example, at one time it was considered normal for men to dominate their wives and for women to take a subservient role in a marriage. Over the course of a few generations, however, courageous women stepped out and demanded something different. The first and second wave feminists created new possibilities for relationships, where each partner stood on equal ground. Initially, this cultural change met with a lot of resistance, and it took a powerful commitment on the part of these women to hold a firm vision of the future.

Today in most parts of our world, what was almost unthinkable just a few generations ago has become the new norm for marital relationships. A new pattern has been created, and young men growing up today in the developed world would never expect their wives to act like domestic servants, any more than young women would expect to blindly submit and obey. The result is that individual women no longer have to fight this battle, because a new cultural pattern has been created — at least for those of us lucky enough to live in parts of the world where this evolutionary change has occurred.

Studying the history of how cultural patterns evolve provides us with evidence on how the evolutionary process works and how new and radical potentials become stabilized and repeatable. Biologist Rupert Sheldrake has studied how such change occurs in the natural world, proposing that information about how systems are structured is stored by nature in what he calls "morphic fields."

> *Systems are organized the way they are because similar systems were organized that way in the past. ... For example, the molecules of a complex organic chemical crystallize in a characteristic pattern because the same substance crystallized that way before; a plant takes up the form characteristic of its species because past members of its species took up that form; and an animal acts instinctively in a particular manner because similar animals behaved like that previously.*[1]

Several scholars, including philosopher Ken Wilber, have suggested that the same principle can be applied to understanding how evolution occurs in human systems. Wilber uses the metaphor of "Kosmic grooves" or "Kosmic habits," and he points out that certain habitual ways of being have been repeated for millennia, cutting a deep "groove" in consciousness that is "as rutted as the Grand Canyon." On the other hand, when we endeavor to create new ways of being and relating that are not habitual, it takes much more effort and commitment. As Wilber explains:

> *This does not mean that individuals cannot pioneer into these higher potentials ... only that those structures are as yet lightly formed, consisting only of the faint footprints and gossamer trails of highly evolved souls who have pushed ahead, leaving gentle whispers of the extraordinary sights that lie before us if we have the courage to grow. These are higher potentials ... they have not yet become structures settled into stable Kosmic habits.*[2]

It takes tremendous commitment to be one of those pioneers, to venture together into territory that has not been charted. For those of us who glimpse such possibilities, mutual commitment is what enables us to stay on course and stabilize these new potentials until they can become established patterns for more and more people.

Staying on the Inside

As we pioneer these new potentials, we must be willing to accept and use whatever arises during our mutual awakening experience, whether it be fear, discomfort, doubt, pain, anger, or rapturous states of bliss that previously were inaccessible. All such new experiences will fuel our forward progress.

As previously discussed, human beings are habituated to seek pleasure and avoid pain. Our egos are oriented toward survival and comfort, and in most conventional relationships the implicit commitment is to *not* disturb each other's egos. Most of us navigate our relationships like soldiers tiptoeing through a minefield, trying to avoid triggering each other's sensitivities. Therefore, the active pursuit of interpersonal breakthroughs can seem counterintuitive and uncomfortable. A mutual commitment to access our higher potentials, as opposed to protecting our base level needs for survival and comfort, is essential if we are to help ourselves and each other stay on course.

I use the term *mutual* commitment because when the stakes are this high — the continued evolution of humanity — it's essential that both parties in the Evolutionary Relationship are equally committed to their own and each other's development as well as the greater value their relationship has for society at large. In some relationships it's sufficient for one person to be fully committed, but in an Evolutionary Relationship, both partners must commit. If one person ceases to develop or fails to fully support the relationship's potentials, the connection changes fundamentally. Thereafter, the relationship's potential is blocked and the commitment is broken.

Jeff Carreira came up with a powerful phrase that captures what it means to be mutually committed. He calls it "staying on the inside" of the relationship. Partners need to agree in advance that when challenges or difficulties are encountered, they will not allow themselves to separate from the relationship in order to deal with or judge the issues that arise. Instead, partners must resolve to stay "inside" the relationship when challenges emerge and together manage the interruption in intimacy.

I remember the first time I introduced this idea in a workshop, because some of my students were moved to tears. The participants reported that they hadn't realized how profoundly affected they'd been by not being able to deeply count on friends and family with whom they felt close. We've all experienced this type of betrayal, when someone we've trusted and opened up to suddenly steps out of a shared commitment, stops communicating, and becomes unavailable. For example, when something goes wrong in a marriage, "staying on the inside" might mean that you don't walk out the door, but instead you tell your partner how you feel, with vulnerability and honesty. You might even confess your fear that the relationship is in jeopardy, but you also can say, "I'm committed to uncovering and discovering what is arising for me and for us. Are you willing to explore this together?"

This is a very different approach, which has the potential to preserve relationships rather than end them, as often happens in our postmodern society. Usually, one partner begins to feel that something is wrong with the relationship and then unilaterally forms a strategy or makes a decision, possibly seeking the advice of a friend rather than discussing the problem with the other partner. Eventually, the disgruntled partner announces that the relationship is over, leaving the other partner "outside" the entire process.

Here's another example: Perhaps you have a friendship that has become difficult and you notice that you're falling into unhealthy patterns or that the relationship is not supporting your growth and development. Rather than taking the time and energy to sit down to share your concerns, you might make excuses to avoid spending time with that friend. Wouldn't it be more satisfying and more deeply loving to recommit to the relationship and allow your friend the opportunity to do the same? Only then can you work together to create more healthy and supportive ways of connecting.

When we cease to stay on the "inside" of a challenging relationship and internally try to craft a solution, we leave the other person feeling helpless and we single-handedly abort the relationship's evolutionary potential.

There always will be challenges in relationships, particularly those that possess evolutionary potential. Therefore, if we truly wish to grow stronger and experience breakthroughs with another human being, we need to forego the option of saying, "I'm not committed anymore" and the tendency to withdraw or take a break. Instead, we need to go toward whatever is there together. We need to stay inside the relationship and remain committed to the highest possibilities for each partner and the partnership.

That doesn't mean we stay in unhealthy relationships, and of course, this process won't work in a relationship where there is not mutual commitment to begin with. But it does mean that we stay in those relationships that have the potential for deep growth — whatever happens. It also means that we learn how to stay in communication with the other person and work through whatever needs to be worked through in order to move forward together.

Real commitment is not something you keep renegotiating; it's a "yes" or "no" decision. Ideally, after you make this commitment, the choice then fades into the background, as an invisible but tremendously powerful foundation for what's to come. Oprah Winfrey expressed this choice beautifully:

Keeping my word is a mandate I live by. I can't tell you the number of times I've committed to doing something, then later wanted to get out of it but ended up doing it anyway because, for me, backing out is never an option. If I agree to do something, the only way I'm not going to do it is if I'm too sick to move.[3]

I've seen the impact of this kind of commitment on my students. For example, the Evolutionary Collective gives people the opportunity to commit for one year at a time. It requires a fairly high level of ongoing participation and engagement. When people enter into the program of study, they make a commitment to stay "inside" the group no matter what arises. Amazingly, in the last few years since we introduced the one-year program, only one person has dropped out! Many people have encountered challenges and faced obstacles, but they navigated them and negotiated solutions within the collective. The result is that my students have experienced personal and interpersonal breakthroughs, and they've become stronger. When we're no longer afraid of being abandoned or losing the commitment of a partner, we find the courage to be open, honest, and vulnerable about less comfortable parts of our experience. I've also noticed that the deeper my student's commitment, the less friction they encounter with others engaged in the process.

A clear, mutual commitment makes the whole journey possible and run smoother, because we forsake the option of constantly renegotiating the basic commitment to the relationship every time we feel uncomfortable or afraid. Once we say "yes" to mutual commitment, we release inner resistance and our energy and attention is freed up. Even more importantly, we make ourselves available to a much greater energy source. I've seen the truth of this over and over again.

In my work, I also have found that it is critical to be "in agreement with yourself" about your commitments. So take the time to agree and align yourself fully with what you have committed to explore with another person. Activate the full power of what you want and are willing to make yourself available to give and receive. Without this intentional alignment, you leave yourself open to all kinds of difficulties and resistance that may eventually undermine what you seek with your partner. Most people don't realize how dangerous it is to leave "options open." That mindset will ensure failure, as you will not be fully aligned with the power of evolution.

To summarize, the second principle of commitment is a "yes" that reveals unseen possibilities, synchronicities, and sources of support. It enables you to see connections and opportunities that can help you move forward and achieve powerful breakthroughs. When you are fully committed, it feels as if you are suddenly plugged into the energy and power of the universe. When you create an Evolutionary Relationship based on mutual commitment, the relational field becomes alive and vibrant. The grace from higher dimensions begins to descend into the relationship in a way that is not possible in an uncommitted context. Truly, an Evolutionary Relationship is sacred.

As you continue reading this book, please remember that without commitment, higher dimensions won't be able to emerge because the vehicle or container that you are trying to create will be insufficient. However, once you learn to stay on the inside of a commitment, you will reach a point where it simply is not possible to separate yourself from that commitment or step out of it. Philosopher Jean Paul Sartre once affirmed this point when he wrote that "commitment is an act, not a word."[4] Further, I would argue that commitment eventually becomes not even an act, but a state of being. It's not a thing you do; it's who you are. To be fully committed is to allow yourself to be shaped by what you are committed to and, eventually, to become one with it.

An Evolving Commitment

The beauty of a commitment to mutual evolution is that although it is clear and wholehearted, it is never fixed or limiting. We are not trapped by the commitment, because within that commitment there is infinite room for expansion and change. In an Evolutionary Relationship, we pay attention to how the relationship is evolving — what form it naturally wants to take, what its potentials are, where it can go. We're not trying to force it to be what we think we need or want it to be, nor to fit our personal agendas. We are sensing together, moment to moment, how the natural design of the relationship is unfolding and how it fits into the larger scheme of life. During this exchange, our commitment isn't just to each other or to a particular result. It's a commitment to evolution itself, which by nature is never fixed and always moving.

Sometimes the form of a relationship changes, sometimes it stays the same. Each relationship has its own nature and you can't simply impose what you want onto it. It's almost like having a child: Your son or daughter will not develop in a healthy, balanced way if you try to shape or dominate him or her to become what you want. The best you can do is stay attuned to your child's needs and potentials and help them grow into their unique destiny. Similarly, you should allow your adult relationship to flourish by giving it all the attention and devotion that it needs and not force it to fit your agenda.

Because relationships possess their own inherent nature, the more deeply you commit to and participate in them, the more attuned you will be to their natural unfolding. With this kind of commitment, it doesn't necessarily mean you will physically "stay together" forever. Even if the parties decide to end a relationship, it's possible to go through this change together, never stepping out of the commitment. Ending a relationship in a compassionate manner is very empowering for both partners, as it is a mutual acknowledgement that the relationship already has fulfilled its highest potentials.

About fifteen years after Peter passed away, I met a wonderful man named Eric. After we'd been dating a while, Eric asked me to marry him and I said "yes." Some months after we got engaged, Eric and I had a conversation about what our commitment meant — what were we committing to and how would that work? We agreed that we weren't committing to a particular form of relationship and that we would hold on to it no matter what happened. We were clear that we were committing to each other and to the truth of our relationship, regardless of how it looked to the outside world. We also committed to stay close, stay related, and stay open and truthful from that day forward.

Eric and I had been married before and shared the experience of having our ex-spouses refuse to stay in connection, and we never wanted to endure that situation again. Eric and I committed to honoring these truths with each other. We both recognized that once two people are connected, they always will be — even if they pretend they aren't. We also agreed that even if our marriage became difficult, we would stay engaged in the mutual awakening process, willing to discover if we needed to work harder or let go. Lastly, we agreed that if the relationship did not work out for some reason, neither of us would claim to be victimized by the other. We were totally committed to the process of Evolutionary Relationship.

Eventually, over the course of four years of intense exploration and intimacy, Eric and I came to a mutual decision not to formally marry. We had some bumpy times through the dissolution of our engagement, but we stayed connected to each other and we kept supporting and discovering new things about one another every step of the way. Today, we still love and respect one other, even though our lives are no longer as intimately connected as they once were.

When I think about how much pain we could have caused each other by not staying on the inside of our relationship, I am grateful for our shared understanding of commitment and what it made possible. Just think how much anguish and anxiety would be alleviated if we could count on every person in our lives to remain honest and transparent even in the face of extreme difficulties. Yet too often the opposite occurs, since lack of true commitment results in fear and judgment and excruciating pain when the other person no longer wants to be inside the challenging situation with us and abruptly exits the relationship.

I believe that if we were more in touch with the truth of our interconnectedness, if we realized that we never truly are separated from people with whom we have developed close bonds, we would learn to consistently relate to one another from the inside. Then, we would stop pretending that it's possible to eschew our parents, children, lovers, friends, mentors, and intimate partners. The Activating Principle of commitment allows us to be fully awake to a truth that has been with us all along: When we try to separate, announce to our partner we are leaving, or pretend we're no longer related to those with whom we've created strong bonds, the only way to manage the pain is to shut down and disconnect from ourselves and our sensitivity to reality and love.

I believe the principle of commitment holds true even when someone we love dies. We work so hard to "get over" the loved one who has left us. For example, when Peter passed away, I thought that if I stayed connected to him and "inside" our relationship, I would never love again. Consequently, I worked hard to "move on" and put a tremendous amount of emotional and psychic energy into letting go of Peter. In the end, though, this approach was a catastrophe. When I finally surrendered to the fact that I still deeply loved Peter and that we were one and always will be, my heart finally gave a sigh of relief because it was the truth. I loved Peter and would remain irrevocably connected to him, even though he wasn't here on Earth to live our love with me.

Since that transformative revelation regarding my deep commitment to Peter, I've had an amazing journey witnessing how my closeness to Peter — long after his death — has assisted me in the unfolding of this work. As Cynthia Bourgeault writes in *Love Is Stronger Than Death*, "Two souls through true love can bond in such a way that they continue to remain one — affecting each other, in communication, and continuing to grow in their love."[5]

EXERCISE:
Practicing Commitment

Always begin with the Mutual Awakening Practice (see the exercise at the end of Chapter Three). The goal is to bring your relatedness into a higher and deeper state of consciousness before you explore the principle of commitment.

Step 1. Discuss and provide answers to the following questions. When forming your answer, each of you needs to be clear about what really matters to you and what you are truly committed to achieving. Hint: There's no point in committing to someone who isn't committed to anything.

- ⌘ Individually, what are you committed to in your life?
- ⌘ Are you committed to achieving a certain level of consciousness?
- ⌘ What is your contribution to the world?

(continued on next page)

Step 2. Next, speak about your reaction to the other person's commitments. Are you willing to get behind and support your partner in his or her commitments (in other words, can you commit to your partner's commitments)? Will you be there to make sure your partner is successful in fulfilling his or her true potentials?

Step 3. The next level of this exercise involves exploring what potentials exist within your new Evolutionary Relationship. At first, just explore what you think is there, without any restrictions or thoughts of commitment. Simply let go and allow all the potentials and possibilities to arise and display themselves. You might want to write your ideas down so you can see what you identify as possible mutual goals. It will help if you let your thoughts flow freely. Try closing your eyes and feeling into the space between you, allowing images and ideas to arise.

Step 4. After letting thoughts on your new Evolutionary Relationship come through, sense which goals feel the most alive, vivid, and real. Explore whether you both are committed to what's been identified as possible in the relationship.

Step 5. If you have unveiled a potential within your relationship that both of you feel you can commit to, then make a pledge to each other to stay on the "inside" of the relationship no matter what — even if you later start to get scared, fear it's not working, or feel a restriction. Commit to one another that you will communicate and work out all challenges. Commit to discover together what it takes to fulfill the identified potentials, without stepping outside the relationship, pointing fingers, or labeling yourself or your partner "wrong." Complete the exercise by being clear that you are *in* and *for* each other — which is shorthand for mutual evolutionary commitment. ෬

For supplementary content, including audios, videos, and exercises, visit: www.EvolutionaryRelationshipsBook.com/bonus

Notes

1   Rupert Sheldrake, *Morphic Resonance: The Nature of Formative Causation*, Rochester, VT: Park Street Press, 2009, p. 3.

2   Ken Wilber, "Excerpt A: An Integral Age at the Leading Edge, Part II: Kosmic Habits as Probability Waves," in *Excerpts from Volume 2 of the Kosmos Trilogy*, http://www.integralesleben.org/uploads/media/01_excerpt_a.pdf, accessed March 12, 2017.

3   "What I Know For Sure: Keeping My Word," *O, The Oprah Magazine*, February 2010, http://www.oprah.com/spirit/Oprahs-What-I-Know-for-Sure-Keeping-My-Word.

4   Quoted by John Gerassi, "Sartre Accuses the Intellectuals of Bad Faith," *New York Times Magazine*, October 17, 1971.

5   Cynthia Bourgeault, *Love Is Stronger Than Death: The Mystical Union of Two Souls*, Rhinebeck, NY: Monkfish Book Publishing, 2014.

CHAPTER SIX
The Third Principle: Truth

I tore myself away from the safe comfort of certainties
through my love for truth — and truth rewarded me.

~ Simone de Beauvoir, *All Said and Done*

The Third Activating Principle of evolutionary mutuality is "truth." I love the term "truth," with all its power and weight, but it's also a term that comes laden with cultural baggage. Therefore, it is important that we take some time to examine what this word means, how its meaning has changed from one era to another, and how context affects is interpretation.

The *Merriam-Webster Dictionary* defines "truth" as "the real facts about something" or that which is "in accordance with fact or reality." Sounds simple enough, right? From this perspective, truth is concrete, measurable, stable, and scientifically verifiable. However, we all know it's more complex than that. For example, in spiritual and religious circles, truth is often used in quite the opposite way — to point to that which is beyond the realm of visible or measurable reality. Truth in this sense means that which is unchanging, absolute — a transcendental, fundamental, or spiritual reality that exists beyond the "false" or impermanent world of relative, changing appearances.

What both of these definitions of truth have in common is that they point to something static and unchanging. By contrast, there's another way of looking at truth, which has become common in our culture over the past hundred years or so. Now, truth often is viewed as something entirely relative. The very notion that anything can be definitively called "true" has been questioned, and many have asserted that all truth is partial — that what we experience as truth are mere perspectives, opinions, and perceptions, or as Friedrich Nietzsche said, "a mobile army of metaphors, metonyms, and anthropomorphisms."[1]

We often hear variations on the phrase, "I have my truth and you have your truth." There is value in discovering your own truth, but there also is a danger in declaring truth to be completely subjective. When I use the term truth, I am neither pointing to a fixed concept nor to an ever-shifting relativism. The simplest definition of truth would be "reality." However, I understand reality to have many levels and dimensions, with each level constituting a deeper truth that coexists with the previous levels, and with each deeper level revealing a new dimension. As a result, reality is evolving — truth is not static, but an evolving spiral of revelation.

As an Activating Principle of evolutionary mutuality, love of truth means the interest and willingness to keep penetrating to ever-deeper levels of reality in any given situation, and the dedication not to pull back for fear of what we might find. We discover truth when we approach what we are inquiring into with an open mind and heart.

What Is Your Relationship with Truth?

Unfortunately, most of us have a conflicted relationship with truth. We live in a world where lies and half-truths are common and part of the normal fabric of our shared reality. Often, we don't want to see the truth about ourselves and others. We think the truth will hurt us, take things away from us, deprive us, or put us into unpleasant situations. If we thought of truth as liberating, we wouldn't spend so much energy manipulating our emotions, avoiding what's real, or trying to protect ourselves from truth.

Because many people avoid the truth, we tend to interact and know each other in a relatively superficial way. This tendency is dangerous, as it makes us gullible and prone to believing the lies others tell us. For example, people often spin distorted realities about who they are and how they want us to perceive them, and we often accept their stories without question. We have grown used to living on the surface and not listening to the parts of ourselves that sense inauthentic realities. Like the townspeople in the parable of the "Emperor's New Clothes," it is easy to buy into a false picture of reality when no one challenges falsehood. It took a small, innocent child to give voice to the truth that the Emperor was not wearing anything. As adults, we need to substitute bravery for innocence and be open to truth.

Yet most adults have a myriad of motivations to avoid truth. Often, our hearts and minds are divided, pulling us in different directions. Desires compete with the love of truth — desires for comfort, safety and security, success, recognition, wealth, and fame. When we are attached to such desires, we resist change and avoid realities that don't fit with how we want things to be.

Lucy, a woman I was working with, once confided in me that she was beginning to sense that something was not quite right in her fifteen-year marriage. Her husband had become distant and secretive. She was worried he might be having an affair, but she didn't want to confront him because she was afraid of finding out the truth and having to deal with the consequences. Terrified of losing him and disrupting the life they'd built together, Lucy spent months living in denial, until finally she couldn't bear it any longer. She reached the point where she wanted to know what was actually going on, no matter what it might mean for their future together. Lucy eventually confronted her husband and, sure enough, her worst fears were confirmed, as her husband was having an affair with a colleague at work.

At this point, Lucy uncovered one level of truth: the facts about what he had been doing, with whom, for how long, and so on. She could have stopped there and, devastated by the betrayal, she might have chosen to walk away from the relationship and try to forget the whole painful episode. But I encouraged Lucy to remain open to a deeper truth and to see if she could uncover exactly why her husband had cheated. Because she had the courage to inquire further, she began to see more layers of truth: the reasons why he cheated, the tensions that had been building in their relationship, the needs they each had been denying and feelings they had not expressed. These truths didn't invalidate or change the fact that he cheated, but they did add more dimensions to the situation.

Once again, I encouraged Lucy to continue to explore the reality of her marriage, and as she did, she encountered still deeper levels of truth. Lucy became aware that she had allowed her own sense of self-worth and value to be dependent on her husband's desire for her. She also discovered how attached she had become to the seeming security and stability of the relationship. Facing these truths brought her closer to her true self than she had been in years, and Lucy felt surprisingly liberated from constantly seeking her husband's approval and clinging to him in an unhealthy manner. Ultimately, Lucy reached a point of restlessness and longing for something more, a new way of being related to her husband that wasn't based on security or the need to belong. Today, Lucy is clear that the breakdown of her marriage was not only her husband's fault. While she doesn't excuse his actions, Lucy knows the marriage had been lacking for both of them for quite a while. Her quest for truth brought her into a more intimate relationship with herself and gave her the courage to face what the future might hold for their relationship.

When we are willing to turn toward truth in this way and let the quest for truth lead wherever it may take us, we are liberated and we discover that ultimately we can trust reality. Why? Because the truth always leads us home — to reality and to ourselves — where we will experience the deep relief of being close to the truth. Also, pursuing truth might even bring us closer to our partner. It doesn't necessarily mean we'll stay together as a couple, but if both partners are willing to be open and discover what is really going on in the relationship, they may be led to a much richer possibility for intimacy. There may be pain along the way and the form of the relationship may change, but if we remain sincere in wanting to discover what is real for both of us and what potentials the relationship can fulfill, our journey of truth will bring us closer to ourselves and to each other.

Think about the areas of your life where you tend to avoid the truth, and ask yourself honestly: *What desires are pulling me away from reality? What do I value more than truth? Is there some truth about myself or my primary relationships that I am avoiding?*

*Truth is liberating but also mandatory if
we wish to attain evolutionary mutuality.
There simply is no other way to reach
heightened levels of self-knowledge,
intimacy, inspiration, and motivation.*

There are a variety of truths that you may be avoiding. They could be spiritual, physical, emotional, intellectual, social, financial or relational truths. For example, you may be in denial about your health, like a nagging pain that you know you should get diagnosed or an unhealthy habit that you are ignoring. Perhaps it is a financial reality that you've been avoiding, or a spiritual need that you're reluctant to admit or explore. Whatever you've been avoiding, if you allow yourself to turn toward it and follow the thread of truth, it will draw you closer. You will be amazed at what opens up.

All of us have experienced the relief of learning a painful truth at some critical moment of our lives. When there's something that we desperately have been hoping is not true — such as a betrayal by a loved one, a diagnosis of a serious illness, etc. — after we uncover the actual truth of the matter, we can begin to let go and experience freedom from the effort it took us to hold reality at bay. As Jesus said, "The truth shall set you free." He didn't say, however, that the truth wouldn't include some pain. If we stay close to reality, we ultimately experience personal freedom, release, and sometimes even joy at finally confronting and allowing truth to guide us.

When we find the courage to stop trying to protect ourselves, our beliefs, and our ideas of who we are, who other people are, and how life is supposed to be, it's exhilarating. We use a tremendous amount of energy when we try to prop up a false picture of reality and manipulate our circumstances to support it, but when we stop holding on, that energy is released. The more we follow the thread of truth, the more we find ourselves falling in love with a liberating closeness to reality.

Love of Truth

The great spiritual traditions teach that we must strive to be undivided in relationship to God and to our own spiritual unfolding, and that we will benefit from placing these higher principles above the things of the world. "Seek ye first the kingdom of heaven," the Bible records. Buddha declared attachment to be the root of all suffering. Such sentiments may sound dogmatic or old-fashioned, but there is a perennial wisdom in these traditions that we would do well to carefully consider.

Moreover, heaven is not a place "up there" in the sky; heaven is the freedom we find when we no longer let base-level desires interfere with our opening and unfolding to the deeper dimensions of reality. So while there is nothing wrong with wanting comfort, safety and security, or even success, recognition, wealth, and fame, we need to take care not to let those desires divide our heart against the truth, thereby compromising our relationship with reality. When we keep our priorities straight, the love for truth comes naturally. It is a subtle beauty, a sweetness of the heart, a passion that is pure and will take us home to our core self.

Consequently, a healthy approach to truth is not driven by a moralistic "should" or some notion of what it means to be virtuous. Truth is not an ideal that we try to live up to or a means to an end. Rather, truth is a strong attractor, like an exquisite piece of art that brings tears to our eyes, or a beautiful sunset that makes our heart beat faster. The heart loves truth.

My students report falling in love with truth, and though they sometimes fight it at first, they usually develop a consuming infatuation for truth. Interestingly, the original meaning of the term "philosophy" was "love of truth." So that makes us all philosophers, not merely in the intellectual sense, but due to a true love of truth. This love arises from the heart and grows in strength by moving ever-closer to reality — a gravitational pull that becomes more powerful as we yield to it.

The love of truth is not utilitarian. Often in life, we're motivated to get somewhere, solve something, or achieve a particular end. The ego always has an agenda, whether it be feeling good or avoiding pain, and no matter what realities must be distorted or avoided in order to do so. The essential self, on the other hand, loves truth for its own sake, regardless of the consequences. Like a lover who is happy just to be in the presence of the beloved, the soul delights in being close to reality. It's not afraid of what will happen or how things will turn out. Therefore, we can't approach truth from a fearful, needy, mental, or practical perspective. We only can reach truth from an open, curious, and selfless state of being.

If your heart sincerely wants the truth, something magical happens. You forget everything else and reality begins to guide you. As you proceed with the work contained in this book, you will fall more deeply in love with truth — the good, the bad, the painful, the beautiful, and the difficult. Whatever truth is revealed, you will want to know it, be close to it, and follow where it leads.

Truth and Curiosity

Curiosity often is viewed as a mental quality, but in fact, curiosity is a movement of the heart and an expression of love. It is the desire to come close to what fascinates and attracts us. It's not about attaining anything; it is a love of something for its own sake. Curiosity is unencumbered by agendas and destinations. While the ego is always trying to grasp and hold onto everything it is drawn to and use it for its own ends, the soul's curiosity is open-ended and always moves closer toward what it loves.

In our culture, we've been taught that it's not really acceptable to be too curious about each other. Remember when you were a child, how fascinated you were by other people? But as you grew older, you probably were told it's not polite to stare, to touch, to wonder, to ask. As we enter the domain of Evolutionary Relationships, we are granted permission to rediscover our natural curiosity about each other.

Curiosity is always possible — in any moment and in response to any situation. Curiosity is the quest for truth, and you may notice that curiosity almost always leads to joy. In fact, the more curious we are, the more natural joy and happiness we experience, as we get closer and closer to that about which we are curious. Curiosity also brings a quality of lightness and playfulness. In an Evolutionary Relationship, our curiosity and interest in the relationship and in each other allows us to expand and open doors to the unexpected and unimaginable truth. Moreover, mutual curiosity ignites the relationship — it's like striking a match in a darkened room. The love of truth has a penetrating quality, since we want to know more, to discover and explore places we haven't been before, together. Curiosity is necessary to fully ignite the depth and creativity possible in Evolutionary Relationships.

Truth and Intimacy

The beautiful thing about love of truth is that it brings us closer to reality, closer to ourselves, and closer to anyone with whom we share this love. As a result, truth gives rise to intimacy. To many people, intimacy just means a generic closeness to another person, but in the way I am defining it, intimacy is an expression of truth because it's an acute closeness to reality and a quality of presence that we can experience personally and together.

On a personal level, intimacy can exist in a moment when you first wake up and become aware of the warmth of daylight surrounding you, the softness of the sheets on your skin, the gentle breeze through an open window. Intimacy can exist in a moment of sitting alone and sipping a glass of wine, by being fully present, immersed in and one with the flavor of the wine and how it is affecting you. It's a kind of inner sensuality that feels tender, alive, and closer than close — a oneness in which you feel all the particulars with a heightened sensitivity.

When I hike the Rockies by myself, I open up to the experience of the air on my skin, the movement of my legs, the inner sense of the muscles in my calves stretching and working, the warmth of the morning sunlight and the beauty of the mountain vistas. It feels like a continuous experience of making love, yet without the erotic element. Everything is unusually vivid, vibrant, substantial, and alive.

The same thing can happen with another person, when two people share a space in consciousness, whether they are playing tennis, sitting quietly side-by-side watching a sunset, or listening to music. They feel intimate with each other, and the reason they feel so close is that they are mutually and simultaneously in contact with reality, rather than lost in their own separate, subjective worlds.

In an Evolutionary Relationship, truth and intimacy are one and the same. When you no longer avoid the truth or resist the full range of your subjective and intersubjective experience and you are truly open to being known by your partner, a new level of intimacy occurs. You can't be truly intimate with yourself or with life or with anybody else if you're not willing to be close to the truth, to reality. If you want intimacy in your life, you first need to wrestle with your relationship to the truth.

Truth and Compassion

Truth is closely related to compassion, as well. Often, compassion is defined as a desire to alleviate someone else's pain, a desire to help humanity. Yet a deeper form of compassion is the ability to be at peace with what is true, no matter how unpleasant or glorious the truth may be. If you study people who are great healers or who have made a difference in the lives of others — Mother Teresa is a prime example — you will find that they have an unusually powerful capacity to accept painful truths and to hold these truths without losing faith or becoming traumatized themselves.

Compassion isn't necessarily about alleviating pain. It is more about rendering pain meaningful. Again, think of Mother Teresa and how she made the entire world aware of India's poverty. Compassion also enables us to be with someone who is suffering without any pretense or separation. Compassion naturally arises from truth and enables us to extend our capacity to be with others and to embrace a greater range of circumstances.

Compassion is a dimension of truth that is commonly misunderstood. Compassion is the ability to share, serve, and connect with others who are in pain and turmoil, by accessing an inner dimension of peace and acceptance based on the context and true reality of the situation.

Developing compassion and the ability to be present and sensitive to others — including their pain, difficulty, or discomfort — is critical to developing Evolutionary Relationships. Only through pure compassion may you stay present as you help other people. I learned this lesson when my mother died. She was a truly great mother, and I loved her deeply. She set the stage for truth when I was very little, and our relationship was one of unconditional love. We always resided in truth together: I was able to be honest with her and whatever I needed to tell her was readily received.

Toward the end of her life, my mother developed dementia, and I never was quite sure how much she understood. She had a bad fall and needed to be hospitalized. After sitting with her for a few days, it became apparent to me that she was in the process of dying. I wasn't sure when it would happen, but I had been present when my father and aunt died, so I knew my mother was in the final phase of her life. As I sat next to her bed and held her hand, I asked, "Mom, do you know what's going on?"

She said, "No." Then she looked at me for an explanation.

I explained to my Mom that she was in the process of dying, which she had seen my father go through the year before. I finished by saying, "I thought you would want to know."

She smiled and said, "Well, I'd better hurry up then," which was so like her!

I laughed and told my mother she didn't need to do anything until she felt ready. I also told her that I was so very grateful that she had brought me into this world, and I promised her that I would stay with her as she left. An intense and overwhelming presence of our long history of love and truth surrounded us. She looked up at me and I felt bathed in her particular kind of motherly warmth.

The next morning when I arrived at the hospital, she was noticeably worse. I was sure I could hear her thoughts: *Since I know I'm dying, I might as well just go ...*

Later that night as I held her hand, my mother took her last breath.

As I reflect on this painful yet poignant moment of my life, I realize that some people might have debated whether it was a good idea to share with a dying parent that the end was near. But I knew that my mother and I had always resided in the truth and that in her final moments she would want nothing less. Remaining truthful with my mother while she passed from this world was not only compassionate, it was the highest tribute I could pay to her and to our relationship. It was an incredibly beautiful, bittersweet, naked experience — a perfect expression of the true love and intimacy we had shared during our lives together.

Compassion for those we love and for those we wish to serve is an important component of truth and one that we need to invite and cultivate in the space between us. Without compassion, we won't feel safe to share or serve each other. As our capacity for compassion and truth grows, we naturally become more accepting, forthcoming, and loving toward ourselves and others.

Turning Toward Pain

Perhaps the most immediate way to explore our relationship with truth is to examine our relationship with pain. All living things have an automatic response of moving toward pleasure and away from pain. Our bodies, emotions, and ego are wired to function that way. Spiritual maturity is the capacity to be present while experiencing either pleasure or pain. This level of consciousness is vast enough to hold intense experiences of joy and ecstasy, as well as emotional and physical pain. In order to become this free, we need to expand our capacity to handle discomfort.

So now let's look at your relationship to pain. Ask yourself: *What's my connection to pain? How do I handle my own pain? How do I relate to the pain of others? What kind of pain can I tolerate or am I willing to accept? And what kind of pain do I avoid at all cost?*

For example, maybe you can handle your own physical pain. And maybe if someone else is physically hurt, you can be with them, no problem. But you might have a harder time dealing with psychological or spiritual pain. Think about how your family of origin dealt with (and perhaps dealt out) pain, by asking yourself: *Did they teach me to suck it up, bear with it and be stoic? Did they minimize my pain or pretend it wasn't there? Did they use pain to manipulate me or other family members? Were they verbally abusive? Were there pretenses or lies being lived in my family?* These are important questions, since we tend to learn how to deal with pain from the people who surrounded us when we were little and our most vulnerable and impressionable.

Thankfully, we can learn to have a more mature and conscious relationship with pain. We can practice just being present with it, by turning toward it instead of running away. We also can try this approach with anything that makes us uncomfortable, such as shame, depression, anxiety, or any other kind of emotional tension that arises in our lives and in our relationships. Moreover, we can practice this with another person — turning toward the truth without trying to figure it out, understand it, or give each other advice. By exploring the truth of our pain, we set the proper foundation for the optimizing force to function. When we face our pain, we create a space in which the most powerful force in the universe can work its magic.

A Channel for the Optimizing Force

Being intimate with the truth of our lives and our relationships is an invitation for the evolutionary impulse to do its work. The evolutionary impulse cannot move through us when we resist, manipulate, or try to avoid reality. In an Evolutionary Relationship, as we begin to mutually share a love of truth and explore it together, that impulse moves us forward, and we find ourselves evolving more quickly together.

It is common for my students to report that after six months of mutual awakening practice, they are amazed at how far they've traveled. The ego tends to want stability and sameness, but the heart delights in being lifted and transformed by the evolutionary impulse. If this optimizing force is allowed to be present, then our development is assured. However, as long as the ego is in charge, it will act like a speed bump on the road to our higher potentials, slowing us down and interrupting the flow of our development.

As we become willing to explore truth together, we must remember to pay attention to what is true for each of us individually and for the relationship. We also must become more courageous and steadfast. This allows the power and beauty of the evolutionary impulse to unfold the potentials of our relatedness with much more intelligence and care than any strategy or plan we could devise. After all, how could we — with our limited sense of self — ever formulate or manipulate our way into a potentiated life?

In the past, our fear was that truth might create disasters and ruin our lives, but what we now discover is that if we follow truth, it will show us a life that is more authentic and aligned with the depths of who we are and our true potentials. Therefore, if we want to achieve our highest destiny, we must let the truth and the optimizing force show us the way.

As you enter this "Garden of Truth" with your partner, you may wonder why you hadn't discovered this way of living and loving before. Just keep yourself facing forward, since your new alignment will lead to an ever-greater surrender and to a real love of the truth — a love that will ignite your relationship and change your lives forever. As you practice loving the truth together, the field between you will open up and reveal the rich possibilities of human interaction — the mystery of what's possible between you. Much of the joy of an Evolutionary Relationship is found in discovering the truth of your partner and seeing the embodiment of their truth unfolding before your eyes. When you are present with each other in this way, you will experience nothing less than Divinity, in the form of each other. May you find yourselves living in the Kingdom of Heaven, together.

EXERCISE:
Exploring the Truth

This exercise can be used to explore anything you are concerned or curious about, whether the issue involves you individually or your relationship. Decide who will share first and approach only one issue at a time. It is helpful to use a timer to keep track of each step.

Step 1. Sit directly across from each other and find the right distance where you feel an easy connection. Close your eyes and meditate for 5 minutes, first centering yourself and then expanding your inner awareness to include your partner.

Step 2. Open your eyes and simply be with each other. Allow yourselves to be open and available to experience whatever arises in the space of your connection. Continue this relaxed posture for 5 minutes.

Step 3. Describe the topic that you have chosen to work with and explain the issue briefly. For example, you might say, "I am having difficulty knowing what to do regarding a problem at work," or "I'm facing a health issue," or "A new opportunity has come to me and I'm not sure how to respond to it."

Step 4. Now, both of you close your eyes and imagine that you are holding the issue on a pillow in the space between you. You may get a feeling or see an image as you imagine holding the issue. Stay open and sense what is there, allowing it to become more vivid. Use your inner senses to taste, touch, see, and hear what is there. Keep your eyes closed as you do this practice, and stay focused and aware of what exists in the space between you as you mutually hold what has been placed on the imaginary pillow.

It's important to remember that the purpose of this practice is *not* to solve the issue or try to reach a desired result. Rather, this exercise is simply an invitation to explore the truth of the situation by turning toward the issue with the heightened focus of your shared attention. Allow the truth to reveal itself to you in whatever way it wants. In order to be open to the emerging

(continued on next page)

truth, both of you will need to let go of your fears, desires, fixed ideas, pre-existing beliefs, and all that you think you "know" about the issue.

Step 5. The person who raised the issue should listen first. Have your partner give voice to what he or she is experiencing while focusing on the issue. What does your partner sense about the issue and how are they experiencing what is there? Don't prejudge your partner's thoughts, just let their description flow and see what unfolds. Stay focused on the issue even though it may be morphing and changing as your partner shares their experience. It's important to stay close to what your partner is actually saying and not hold on to what you began with.

When your partner is complete, then it's your turn to tune in and share your sensing. You can continue to loop back and forth like this for 10 to 15 minutes.

Step 6. Spend the last 5 minutes speaking "from" the issue itself. What is the issue experiencing? For example, if a money concern was raised, speak directly from the sense of frustration or feeling of lack. If it was a problem of procrastination, speak directly from the procrastination. Hint: This step is similar to the step in the Mutual Awakening Practice when you ask "What are WE experiencing?"

When you are complete, sit for a few minutes in silence with your eyes closed and be present to the influence of whatever has happened during the practice for you individually and for the relationship. Then open your eyes and share your experience and any realizations or insights you may have gained.
CB

For supplementary content, including audios, videos, and exercises ,
visit: www.EvolutionaryRelationshipsBook.com/bonus

Notes

1   Friedrich Nietzsche, translated by Walter Kaufmann, *The Portable Nietzsche*, New York, NY: Penguin Books, 1977.

CHAPTER SEVEN
The Fourth Principle: Trust

Ultimately, there can be no complete healing
until we have restored our primal trust in life.

~ Georg Feuerstein

Do you ever think about the air that you breathe? My guess is, probably not, unless it's polluted or in short supply, in which case it comes to your attention immediately. If you climb a mountain and reach a high altitude where the air is thin, you'll suddenly become aware of every breath in a new way. If you get out of a plane in Beijing, where the smog is worse than Los Angeles was back in the 1980s, you'll very quickly become conscious of what's moving in and out of your lungs. But for most of us, until it's compromised in some way, the air we breathe is something we almost never think about, even though it's fundamental to life.

The same principle applies to trust. Trust is absolutely fundamental to all relationships, yet most of the time we are not aware of it … until it breaks down. As the old saying goes, "You don't know what you've got till you lose it." Anyone who has ever experienced betrayal in a close relationship knows that trust, once broken, is difficult and sometimes impossible to repair. Something that was taken for granted suddenly becomes conspicuous due to its absence.

Trust is foundational. It is the invisible foundation on which all our relationships rest: our relationship to ourselves, to life, and to each other. Trust is in the background shaping the way we relate in every moment, the way we interact with everything we encounter. As you will discover in this chapter, there is a fundamental kind of trust that — if you were to recover your contact with it fully — would return you to a state of consciousness in which you could relax on the deepest levels. A fundamental soul alignment would occur and your life would naturally unfold in a way that would allow you to develop and express your highest potentials.

On a more practical note, business expert Stephen M. R. Covey writes that "trust impacts us 24/7, 365 days a year. It undergirds and affects the quality of every relationship, every communication, every work project, every business venture, and every effort in which we are engaged. It changes the quality of every present moment and alters the trajectory and outcome of every future moment of our lives — both personally and professionally."[1]

The importance of trust cannot be overstated. If trust is missing, we move into a different world, one in which we cannot relax and have little power. Carly, a woman who attended one of my recent workshops, received a critical insight about trust. She realized she had been waiting for it to feel safe to trust. "I now think of trust as something I decide to give — an investment in being related," she said afterward.

When we engage in Evolutionary Relationships, it is absolutely essential that we become awake to and masterful in the domain of trust. We must learn that trust is not a passive, background experience, but an active, catalytic ingredient that sparks the creative potentials inherent in the relationship. This Fourth Activating Principle actually consists of three levels of trust, each of which is an essential component. Mastering these three levels of trust will give us a set of refined distinctions that will enable us to see what fosters trust and what disrupts it. Remember: Trust is an elusive principle to work with, because when it's fully present it's invisible. Making trust more visible by becoming aware of its subtle distinctions will empower us, not only in our relationships but in every arena of life.

Three Levels of Trust

When embarking on an Evolutionary Relationship, there are three levels of trust we need to study, each of which must be consciously cultivated and nurtured:

1. **Basic Trust.** This is the most fundamental and powerful level of trust. I was introduced to this dimension of trust by A.H. Almaas, a teacher I studied with, who has a profound and nuanced understanding of the dynamics of basic trust. Basic trust is not an attitude or a feeling; it's a fundamental ground of being that rests upon our souls' original experience of non-separateness, of oneness, of knowing that we are one with existence. It is based in the deeper reality of who we are, beyond our identification with being a separate body and a separate ego. It's the primal trust of knowing we are one with the essential goodness of existence and can never be separated from that oneness.

2. **Relative Trust.** This is the kind of trust we most commonly experience — the trust between ourselves and other people. Relative trust depends on our integrity, our intentions, our behaviors, our humility, and our capabilities.

3. **Generative Trust.** This is the kind of trust that becomes possible in an Evolutionary Relationship. Generative trust is based on mutual commitment, and it includes the recognition that we will have breakdowns in trust, but that when we do, we will discover what is needed to restore and generate greater trust. It also is a commitment to continue to develop our capacity to relax into basic trust, together and individually.

All three of these levels of trust are integral to forming and sustaining an Evolutionary Relationship. Let's take a closer look at each type of trust, and I'll share with you some contemplations and practices that can help you to engage with this elusive but essential principle.

The First Level: Basic Trust

Basic trust is one of the most powerful and transformative principles we can engage with. It is not something we *do*; it is something we *are* — a foundational awareness of our intrinsic oneness with the essence of life itself.

The term "basic trust" originates from the field of developmental psychology. The 20th Century psychologist Erik Erikson, who conducted an enormous amount of research on how children develop, used the term to describe "the general sense that the world is predictable and reliable" — a confidence that is found in children who have secure attachments with their parents. A.H. Almaas, whose work was informed by the research of Erikson and others, explored and expanded on the spiritual dimensions of this concept with his unique blend of psychological and mystical insight. He describes basic trust as:

> *[A]n unspoken, implicit trust that what is optimal will happen, the sense that whatever happens will ultimately be fine. It is the confidence that reality is ultimately good; that nature, the universe, and all that exists are of their very nature good and trustworthy; that what happens is the best that can happen. Basic trust is a non-conceptual confidence in the goodness of the universe, an unquestioned implicit trust that there is something about the universe and human nature and life that is inherently and fundamentally good, loving, and wishing us the best.*[2]

Basic trust, as the psychologists recognized, profoundly affects the way in which we develop, from the moment we come into this world and throughout our lives. If we are grounded in basic trust, we tend to grow and develop fairly naturally and we remain oriented toward the soul's development. If basic trust is missing, however, we develop stronger and more fixated egos, which cause us to be more defensive, vigilant, and controlling.

Ironically, people who are connected to basic trust have no conscious awareness that they are more relaxed and trusting — it's simply their natural state of being. In Almaas's words, you have basic trust if you know that "even if you fall, you will be held. If you let go, things will be okay. If you let yourself not know, you will be guided. If you do not manipulate, you will be taken care of in a way that is appropriate for you."[3]

We are born with basic trust – an innate confidence that we will be protected, nurtured, and loved. We also share an undifferentiated consciousness that we experience with and as the universe.

Basic trust is something all of us are born with. When we first come into this world, we are connected to this dimension of love, which Almaas calls the "living daylight." He describes the living daylight as a "tender and loving presence, experienced as the origin of all states of consciousness, as well as the origin of everything."[4] The living daylight is likely the first boundless or cosmic dimension that we experience. Later in life, when we have a spiritual opening, we recapture the living daylight. Once again, we feel the universe as luminous, alive, animated, and pervaded with consciousness, intelligence, light, and love. Being in touch with this presence is what gives rise to basic trust, as Almaas explains:

> *If this loving presence is seen as the true nature of everything that exists, the universe is seen as benevolent since it is made up of benevolence, and is therefore something you can trust. ...*
> *If the universe as a whole and everything in it is pervaded by, is composed of, and is an expression of, this fundamental loving presence, it is natural that you would feel relaxed and trusting, with the sense that you will be taken care of and that things are going to turn out okay.[5]*

When we're born, we are bathed in this living daylight. We are part of it and we experience its goodness and love directly. As a result, we are relaxed, even though helpless. We assume we will be held, nourished, protected, understood, and loved. It's a preverbal, pre-conscious conviction — like the assumption of a flower that there will be sunlight and rain. We feel at home in the universe and trust that this is our natural condition.

As we develop, though, we begin to lose this effortless connection with our true nature, and with it our basic trust. We move from the living daylight into a more shadowy world. Why do we lose it? Because at some point in our early development, most of us no longer feel held and supported by existence. Erikson associated this "holding" solely with our parents or caretakers, but psychologist Donald Winicott, whose work I mentioned in Chapter Four, took a more comprehensive approach to what he called the "holding environment" that surrounds a young child. Winicott also includes in the holding environment our mother's or caretaker's moods, feelings, psychological states, and emotional availability or lack thereof. He also takes into account the emotional climate in our home, the tensions that might arise as a result of parental or sibling conflict, financial difficulties, illness, or even social or political unrest in the broader culture. Consequently, our holding environment also includes the level of chaos in our home and any lack of stimulation.

All these factors add up to an experience for the child that is more or less "holding." If the environment is supportive, the child will feel cared for, protected, understood, and loved, in such a way that his or her consciousness — which is unformed, fluid and changeable — can organically and naturally grow on its own. The young soul is like a seedling. It needs the right soil, nutrients, and weather conditions to grow into a strong tree. If unexpected storms sweep through, or a drought leaves the land barren and dry, the tree will grow stunted and contorted. In the same way, a baby needs an environment that is consistent, attuned to its needs, and supportive of those needs in a way that the child experiences as relatively effortless and natural. Babies can handle certain amounts of frustration and some degree of challenge, but their consciousness will begin to contract if they encounter events that are too extreme, disruptive, or constantly difficult.

When babies don't feel "held" by their environment, they attempt to hold themselves and compensate to protect themselves. Their energy and focus becomes absorbed with trying to get what is missing. For example, if a baby is hungry and not being fed often enough, she will scream and cry to get someone to pay attention. Another baby might not be able to digest too much food at one time, and need less food but more often. And another baby may be physically sensitive and contract and tense up when held in a way that is too rough or unconscious.

In all of these examples, the baby's experience of oneness and connectedness gives way to a sense of separation, stress, and mistrust. The environment no longer "just works" and the baby begins to feel the need to "make it work" for herself. The baby automatically contracts in response to having to find a way to get what she needs. She no longer can relax, and eventually she focuses all her attention on getting what she needs. This is when the structures of the ego begin to form and become fixed in ways that help the baby learn coping skills to navigate an unfriendly universe. The baby's energy turns toward survival, the natural unfolding of the soul is interrupted, and the development of the ego takes over.

To varying degrees, this experience of separation and mistrust happens to all of us, although in some areas of life, you may find yourself naturally relaxed and trusting. You don't really think about that part of your life working, it just does. You might feel completely at ease in your relationships, your work, your financial affairs, or your health. My experience is that those aspects of my life which I find effortless are in the "background," whereas those situations which involve tension and a lack of basic trust are in the "foreground."

It's easy to identify the areas of your life which lack basic trust: Just think about those parts of your life that seem to never work, no matter how much effort you expend in trying to create change. You may feel that if you stop paying close attention and doing what you can to control things, that part of your life would fall apart. You also may experience feelings of anxiety, loneliness, or frustration in these areas of life — even to the extent that you feel a little crazy. For some people, issues around food or health express this lack of basic trust, and no matter how much they struggle, they can't seem to find a simple and straightforward relationship to what they put into their bodies or the way they exercise. For others, it might be a struggle with sleep or sex. These are fundamental areas of life that we intuitively know should be simple, yet they can consume much of our attention.

When areas of our life don't work, we start to judge ourselves, our failures, and our obsessions. We also mistrust our ability to handle life's situations naturally and appropriately. The ego then manifests as a mistrust of life, and it develops skills and strategies to support our conviction that life isn't going to work for us unless we make it work. Some people become overly selfish and preoccupied with trying to make sure that their needs are met. Other people express a lack of basic trust by trying to control everything — their inner experience, their bodies, their relationships, and life circumstances. As a result, their characters become rigid, as they resist being influenced or affected by others and attempt to dominate others or outsmart the universe. Such people may appear very disciplined or motivated, but when you look beneath the surface, there is a lot of tension driving their behavior. Still others may become defensive, isolated, and emotionally withdrawn.

It is important to understand that until basic trust is restored, the strategies of the ego will become more and more developed. Even when we strive for self-improvement and personal growth, we unconsciously may be acting from a contraction of the ego. However, if we focus on restoring basic trust, we might find that those sticky areas of life will take care of themselves. We then can rebuild a natural relationship with our bodies, our time, our relationships, and our life.

From the perspective of our evolutionary potential, the most damaging effect of lack of basic trust is that it holds us back from the unfolding edge of our development. Without basic trust, we just can't afford to live on the edge. We're too frightened, and have too many reasons to justify holding on and holding back. To develop higher levels of human development, we need to let go of our current sense of identity and move beyond aspects of life that we have outgrown. To reach our potential, we must leap into the unknown.

*The good news is that basic trust
is recoverable and egoic patterns that
dampen trust can be healed.
Moreover, basic trust is not something you have
to create, since it is inherent in your being.*

As you begin to reawaken your relationship to basic trust, your creativity will return. Suddenly, you can afford to let go and take risks, as the unfolding edge of life becomes compelling rather than frightening. You will feel an unquestioned confidence that the universe will provide what is necessary. Even when you stumble or encounter setbacks, you will have the resilience to pick yourself up and keep going. You will experience a fundamental resilience and know that you are in a dance with life itself. Thereafter, once you rediscover basic trust fully from a place of maturity, you will be relaxed, internally and externally, and able to spontaneously take action. Areas that were a struggle will begin to flow more naturally, and your soul's development will unfold organically, guided and empowered by the optimizing force of life.

This kind of trust is what we see in the great saints and in people who undergo powerful spiritual awakenings. They have re-embraced basic trust and their level of surrender has reestablished contact with this consciousness. A friend of mine who was close to Mother Teresa once shared with me what the great Saint said to her: "Whatever comes, you accept it. If God makes you a king, you accept being a king. If God makes you a beggar, you accept being a beggar." That's the beauty of basic trust: It is not relative or conditional to circumstances. This kind of trust is what the saints refer to as "perfect faith." It's a level of spiritual maturity and purification where you trust the Divine completely. There is no separation anymore between you and God. You are held by, surrendered to, made of and inside God, and you know that whatever happens is an expression of Divine love.

When you are in touch with the core and essential nature of life and you know you are not separate from it, your trust no longer is shaken by changing events that occur on life's surface. Your sense of fundamental safety and wellbeing is part of the fabric of your experience. Even if events of the moment are disappointing, painful, or disastrous, you know that you can handle them and that things will work out for the best. This doesn't mean that you stop engaging in positive efforts to change and evolve, but you do so from a place of trust and connection with life. You are energized by the optimizing force that wants to help unfold your highest potential, and you are free to act powerfully and courageously in the world.

The Second Level: Relative Trust

Relative trust is conditional, and it's the more familiar kind of trust that we experience in our day-to-day relationships. Unlike basic trust, which is unconditional, relative trust is shaped by various factors that are present in our relationships and in each of us as individuals. We've all experienced the difference between a relationship where there is a high degree of trust and one where trust is lacking. High-trust relationships can survive turmoil. Partners can make mistakes, say the wrong thing, and still not lose each other. However, in a low-trust relationship you have to be careful, since even a small mistake may be misinterpreted and lead to one partner terminating the relationship.

While basic trust is the most important kind of trust and foundational to everything, relative trust is tremendously significant when it comes to our interactions with other human beings. In the context of Evolutionary Relationships, we must be willing to embrace the reality of how the conditional domain of trust works. A higher order of relating relies on partners being able to manage greater levels of complexity. In order to do this, we need to restore our connection to unity and basic trust, while at the same time conscientiously developing the characteristics and qualities in the relative world that allow us to be more trustworthy, individually and together.

Remember, trust is always the invisible context for our relationships. Even when we are dealing with more concrete interpersonal dynamics, trust exists in the background, informing and shaping the ways we show up with each other. When there is flow, love, or heightened creativity blossoming in a relationship, trust exists in the background. When there are misunderstandings, disruptions, and various forms of separation, mistrust is present. When trust breaks down, the relationship starts to diminish, and if more trust is lost, the relationship will become even more difficult, until eventually there is no relationship at all. People may elect to stay in a relationship that has no trust, but in actuality the relationship is dead.

Despite the indispensable role that relative trust plays in our interpersonal relationships, we're often not very conscious of the particular elements that influence how much (or how little) we trust each other. The following qualities will shed light on what needs to be present for trust to deepen and permeate our relationships. These are by no means the only factors that influence trust, but in my work over the past few decades, I've found that these are the most important ones.

Integrity

Integrity is a key element when it comes to relative trust. When I use the term integrity, I don't mean a moral stance. It's not about rules, compliance, ethics or religious commandments. Initially, it's about living from and being true to your values and ideals. Ultimately, it's about being true to yourself and to your essential nature. People with integrity live lives that are congruent. They "walk their talk." They say what they mean and mean what they say. Their actions reflect the values and ideals they stand for, and as their integrity and development deepen, they live from the most awakened dimension of self. The more a person lives in a way that is consistent with their stated values, the more we instinctively trust them.

Integrity is a complex concept, because it can mean different things to different people at different levels of development. To dig a little deeper into the distinctions I wish to make, let's refer back to Robert Kegan's developmental model, which we examined in Chapter One. We can use Kegan's model to highlight how integrity evolves through the three major stages of adult development. For example, a person who reaches Kegan's "socialized mind" stage will view integrity as conforming to the rules and mores of the social context in which they live. This kind of integrity is strong in religious cultures and the military. So long as the values of the culture they're conforming to are wholesome, such people can be very trustworthy. However, when those values are less healthy or have become outdated and inappropriate for a changing world, people who follow them blindly become difficult to trust.

For a person who evolves beyond the socialized mind level and becomes "self-authoring," integrity means living in a way that is congruent with one's consciously chosen values and ideals, and giving and keeping one's word accordingly. At this level, integrity is more flexible and less rigid. For example, if a person at this level needed to break his word for some reason, he still would have integrity if he honestly communicates why he cannot honor the promise and is willing to deal responsibly with the consequences. Such a person can maintain integrity as he grows, if he is willing to clean up the messes he makes when he falls short. Therefore, as we grow, our values and our sense of who we are, why we're here, and what really matters can expand and change, so long as we constantly stretch to remain congruent.

A new form of integrity emerges when a person awakens to the next stage of development, what Kegan calls the "self-transforming mind." Here, a person's sense of identity becomes more fluid, in touch with a deeper source of self, and conscious of the interconnectedness of all life and existence. Integrity at this level means living congruently with one's true self and the interpenetrating awareness of one's connectivity to everything else. As a result, our actions are informed by a larger context than just our own agendas.

As we discussed in Chapter One, Evolutionary Relationships tend to occur between people who are moving into the self-transforming stage of development. Therefore, in an Evolutionary Relationship this understanding of integrity is particularly important. We begin to listen not simply to socialized expectations or self-authored beliefs and values, but to the evolutionary impulse itself and to the guidance and direction we receive together in relationship. Integrity, in this context, looks like surrender and alignment. But of course, as in all development, this highest level "transcends and includes" what comes before — to borrow a term from Ken Wilber — so it also embraces an understanding of what's culturally acceptable and a commitment to live consistently with our own deepest values.

Humility

In order to live with integrity and trust, we also must integrate the critical element of humility. A humble person is more concerned about what *is* right than about *being* right. Such a person is willing to see the truth, to be open to new information, and to release the desire to defend outdated positions.

When we are lost in pride, we refuse to look at where we might lack integrity, because such an inquiry challenges our self-image. When we identify with a particular way of seeing ourselves and our world, our sense of security is dependent on that view of reality. We can't afford to be open to change because it feels potentially threatening. Therefore, we resist change and act from defensiveness, arrogance and denial. Not surprisingly, people will instinctively mistrust us as a result.

> *From a developmental standpoint, we face a formidable challenge when we embrace humility, since it replaces our personal pride, needs, and agendas. Humility requires an elevated desire to grow beyond our self-authoring stories and our self-determined limits.*

Pride also is devastating to a relationship. If there's a relationship that you're struggling with, ask yourself honestly: *Is pride making my relationship unworkable? Am I holding on to fixed ideas, convinced that I already know how things are? Or am I open and humble enough to be willing to grow?* "Stonewalling" may be defined as an unwillingness to listen to and be influenced by others. Undoubtedly, stonewalling is one of the main factors in divorce.

When we move into the self-transforming stage, it becomes easier for us to access higher states of acceptance, willingness, joy, and peace. In order to be aligned with the more fluid and interpenetrating consciousness of this stage of development, we naturally become more open and less attached to a fixed sense of self. This new consciousness results in an effortless kind of humility, since we are attuned to what actually works in any given situation.

Expectations

Implicit and explicit expectations also deeply affect relative trust. For example, if you are married your spouse has certain expectations of you, and you probably have a sense of what they are, even if the expectations have not been expressly stated. Expectations represent another invisible dimension that fundamentally shapes our visible world. To have integrity and be considered trustworthy, you need to be aware of and live up to the reasonable expectations of others (or make it very clear if you are *not* going to do so). Otherwise, you will compromise your integrity in that relationship and the other person will not trust you. More importantly, the relationship will not work.

Notice if you have resistance to the idea that we need to meet the reasonable expectations of others. Does it make you feel uncomfortable? Generally, we don't want to be responsible for the expectations of other people, relationships, and situations. However, when it comes to illuminating trust in relationships, we need to be cognizant of the hidden domain of what is between us. Human beings always have expectations, and whether or not we fulfill them has an impact on our relationships. You may be unwilling to assume responsibility for other people's hidden expectations, but you can be responsible for sharing your own expectations, and for telling them which of their explicit expectations you are willing to honor and which ones you are not.

For example, as a mother I could feel the expectations that my son had of me. These were normal for a small boy, and they would have been reasonable if I'd been like my mother — someone who didn't work, who had time to cook dinner every night, and whose sole attention was being a wife and mother. However, I became a mother during a different era and I was a different person. My life was devoted to the work of awakening and transformation.

When my son was six years old, we had a delightful conversation about our relationship. I told him how much I loved him and that he could count on me to be there and support him no matter what. I also told him that I probably wouldn't bake cookies, wear an apron, or be like Grandma. We would share other things. We would go on adventures which would help him learn about the world and discover the many possibilities for his life. With his six-year-old insightfulness, he said I was a "cool mom" and smiled and hugged me. That conversation saved me from years of comparing myself to an inner standard and to expectations that I never wanted and really had no commitment to meet. Instead, I was able to relate to my son fully and with integrity. I also had the beautiful experience of parenting him in a way he could trust and in a manner that allowed me to be myself and trust my absolute commitment to him.

Consider one of your close relationships in this light: *What are the expectations the other person has for you? Are you living up to those expectations? What is your relationship to those expectations? And which of those expectations need to be clarified?* It is important to be clear with others and take a stand for what you can and cannot be counted on to be or do for them. Additionally, expectations get out of alignment sometimes, such as when one partner expects life to continue without interruption despite internal or external changes. It is better to explicitly acknowledge changes and discuss whether that means expectations need to change too. Sharing expectations — especially if one partner is shifting — will restore trust.

Intentionality

Another key element of relative trust involves our intentions and motives. Some people are extremely sensitive and aware of their intentions, while others remain mostly unconscious. If you want to be trusted, know what your real intentions are, share them with your partner, and assume responsibility for meeting them. However, if you love someone who is either unaware of their motives or who has a hidden agenda, you won't be able to trust them, not just because of their hidden intentions but also due to their lack of self-knowledge. This is another area where pride can get in the way of trust. If one partner is attached to upholding a particular self-image, there won't be an accurate or humble assessment of their intentions. If you want to discover their true motives, you may ask: *"Why are you doing this? What are you seeking from me? Why do you care about this?"* Eventually your partner's real intention may be revealed.

Fortunately, most people are intuitively aware of their partner's intentions. You can be in relationship with someone who has a lot of integrity, but if his intentions are self-serving, you won't trust him. Selfishness instinctively causes mistrust, while the motive that inspires the greatest trust is care and love. The consciousness of mutuality — where we are sensitive to and interested in what works for both partners individually, the relationship, and the greater whole — naturally inspires growing trust.

With any relationship, it is important to discover whether both partners' intentions are aligned. If your visions are not the same, you'll want different things from the relationship and you'll likely have problems with mistrust. Again, it is best to make your intentions explicit. To determine if your visions are aligned, simply ask each other: *What's your vision for us? What's your vision for life?* With aligned visions and a reasonable amount of integrity, it's easy to build trust because both partners are committed to the same intentions. Even if you stumble, there still will be trust and room to grow together.

In the context of creating an Evolutionary Relationship, full disclosure of intentions is even more critical. You will need to have detailed conversations about each of your personal visions and whether together you have a shared vision to which you can mutually surrender. If so, then the evolutionary impulse is inviting you to enter into a powerful life together. Over time, you will learn to place your attention on allowing that dynamic force to move you. As this happens, you also will develop an awareness of the future pulling you both forward, which is a stage of your Evolutionary Relationship that we will explore in the final chapter of this book.

Capability

Another factor that can strengthen or weaken relative trust is capability. Sometimes we are quite sincere in our intentions and have high integrity, but we simply don't have the capabilities or skills to follow through. As a result, it's natural for people not to trust us in that area, particularly if we're unaware of our limitations due to an inflated self-image. If we have a grandiose idea that we are developed in a certain domain, when actually we lack the necessary knowledge or skills, people will be hesitant to trust us — and for good reason. Therefore, if we don't have clarity or the ability to accurately and objectively assess our capacities, we will be viewed as less trustworthy.

Of course, we are all growing and developing. Consequently, if you are honest about the limits of your capacities, those limits themselves do not have to be an obstacle to trust. But if you continue to pursue endeavors where you lack capability, you need to ask yourself: *Am I being honest about my capacities? Am I making the effort to develop them? Do I keep growing to meet the needs of the situation? Am I excited about learning and contributing new skills? Or do I have a sense of entitlement and complacency?*

Capacity questions most often play out in work relationships, but they can arise in friendships as well. Some people lack the social skills needed to maintain friendships. They may not have been exposed to healthy relationships, they may lack listening skills, or they may feel too vulnerable to share their thoughts appropriately. Human beings are complex creatures, and our development never occurs evenly. Inevitably there will be some areas in which each of us is highly developed, and other areas in which we lack skill and confidence. When we consciously try to build a trusting relationship, it's very important to be aware of these natural imbalances. Otherwise, we may be taken aback when someone who seems highly developed and capable in one way appears clumsy and unconscious in another.

In an Evolutionary Relationship, we need to pay attention to the different capacities of each partner and to those we find lacking, so that we can develop together in needed ways. One partner may need to develop more sensitivity, empathy, or intuitive capacities. The other partner may need to work on the ability to hold different perspectives at once, the capacity to experience higher states of consciousness, or the capability to bear intensity with maturity. If we tune in together to the particular capacities that our relationship needs in order for us both to fulfill our highest potentials, the relationship will flourish. Simply pay attention to developing capacities together and make it part of the relationship's purpose. This is how we build trust — through mutual awareness of what capacities are present, missing, or need attention.

Results or Effectiveness

The final element I want to discuss also relates to capabilities. Specifically, partners need to focus on their effectiveness at following through on their capacities and the results they produce together. I'm sure you have had the experience of being in a relationship with someone who is fully capable of performing, but fails to deliver, time and time again. It's hard to trust someone like that. For example, perhaps your partner has a deep capacity for creativity but rarely keeps her end of the bargain when you engage in shared projects. You know she has the skills and abilities, but her track record is one of half-finished projects and frustrated partners. Or perhaps you're in a relationship with someone who is very enthusiastic but hasn't proven himself yet. He's had several failed relationships, so it's natural that you would question how much you can trust him. In order to be trustworthy, it's not enough just to have the capabilities or the understanding of what's needed — you also need to deliver results.

Trust comes from finishing what you start and having a good track record over time. When people see the outcome of your capacities in concrete, measurable ways, their trust in you will grow.

We now have covered integrity, humility, expectations, intentions, capabilities, and results. Use these qualitative factors to help you understand your relationships, particularly those where trust may be lacking. If you notice that a particular relationship has diminished in some way — it may have become smaller, less relaxed, or decreased in its sense of potential — think about whether any of these factors may be responsible. Is a lack of integrity, pride, a selfish motive, or a misalignment of visions eroding trust in the relationship? Is there some capability that's missing or lack of a particular skill? Or maybe mistrust is being fueled by a shortage of results. Is one of you unreliable, promising things that are never delivered or falling short of reasonable expectations? Once you identify what's missing in the relationship, it can be addressed. But first you need to pinpoint exactly what is going on so you're left with more than the gut reaction, "I don't trust you anymore." Take the time to explore each of these factors and seize the power to restore your relationship.

The Third Level: Generative Trust

The third level of trust is what I call "generative trust," and it is based on commitment and mutuality, themes we've been exploring in previous chapters. Generative trust is a more rare and emergent potential that is found in relationships based on the Eight Evolutionary Principles. This type of trust is "generative" because it's not a trust that makes us feel secure. Rather, it is a trust that gives rise to new and evolving potentials which may shake us to our core.

In order to enact generative trust, we first need to establish that there's a commitment and a willingness to "stay on the inside" of the relationship, no matter what happens. We must agree in advance not to step outside of the relationship or point fingers at each other. When both parties are deeply committed in this way and willing to be responsible for the relationship and for discovering what it needs, generative trust can emerge.

Too often, we approach new relationships with a blind or naïve trust, in which we assume that nothing will go wrong. Then we're shocked when something does go wrong, we throw up our hands, and we step outside of the relationship, feeling betrayed. Generative trust does not rely on everything being perfect or stable or unbroken — quite the opposite. It's a trust in the commitment that's been made, knowing that there inevitably will be breakdowns along the way. Generative trust is ongoing, dynamic, and big enough to embrace the mistakes that we'll make as we strive to truly evolve together and evolve the relationship.

Generative trust embraces the dynamics of basic trust and relative trust: healing our distance from the "living daylight," building integrity, clarifying intentions, expanding capacities, both personally and in the relationship. Generative trust is an essential ingredient for relationships that seek to continuously evolve. When we engage in this way, we're not trying to keep things safe, so we expect a bumpy ride. We use any breakdowns that occur to discover what is missing so we can create a more profound level of commitment and relatedness.

In an Evolutionary Relationship, we agree to extend trust first. Then, if it gets broken, we extend trust again, genuinely, in an attempt to understand together what went wrong. Was it integrity? Was it competence? Was it some element of our commitment to one another that wasn't strong enough?

We want to get to the heart of what happened so that we become even more capable of trust, and in so doing, we establish a stronger and stronger base for the Evolutionary Relationship and for evolution itself.

This process may sound straightforward, but actually it's quite rare. It's very hard for most of us to extend trust again once it's been betrayed. In most relationships, the moment trust is broken we begin an automatic ratcheting down of expectations. We become cynical or disillusioned, and we begin to protect ourselves by expecting less. Cynicism is an enemy of trust, along with selfishness.

Cynicism is a general distrust of others' motives. Selfishness is the unwillingness to give more than you get. When these insidious attitudes creep in, the potential of the relationship diminishes and its scope becomes narrower, until we are relating in such a small space that nothing truly extraordinary can happen between us anymore. At best, the relationship is superficially functional, because the moment we stop being open and vulnerable with each other, a sense of separation begins. We start to relate to each other as objects and the potential for having an Evolutionary Relationship has ended.

The reality is that all relationships suffer from mistrust at one time or another. Evolutionary Relationships are not free from mistrust either, but they "quarantine" it within the greater field of generative trust. By containing mistrust, partners are able to see whatever is there, probe it, and heal the mistrust without the relationship breaking apart.

What gives you the strength and courage to extend your trust in an Evolutionary Relationship is the knowledge that it's not just for your personal gain. Despite the fact that humans are imperfect and not always trustworthy, you feel compelled to build the relationship, for the sake of your partner and for the sake of humanity. A primary goal is to discover how human beings can continue to generate trust. If we as a species are to continue evolving, we have to develop our ability to keep reconnecting with each other and trusting each other at deeper and deeper levels.

Once your commitment is established and anchored in this sense of a higher purpose, you will possess the fortitude to keep going. When two people are fully committed, the possibilities for what can be created together are extensive. In conventional forms of relating, we learn how to get along and accept each other as we are. In an Evolutionary Relationship, we're always reaching for who we can be and what our union can express. We begin with a shared vision of what is possible for the relationship, and eventually, as we surrender more and more to the evolutionary impulse at the center, it guides us far beyond any vision that we could imagine. That is why trust, in this context, is generative: It is the invisible force that relaxes and opens us to the power of the optimizing force of life that brings forth our higher potentials.

Human beings are extraordinary. When we commit to each other and to what's possible, the world changes. To me, human relationship is an art form. There is incredible beauty, richness, and depth that can be activated if we turn toward each other with trust and dedicate ourselves to the higher dimensions that welcome us. Unimaginable potentials seek our participation and cooperation to facilitate "Heaven on Earth." In the exercises which follow, I invite you to activate trust and allow yourself to be carried forward by the optimizing force of life.

EXERCISE 1:
Restoring Basic Trust — An Individual Practice

To restore basic trust, first identify the root of the loss of trust in a particular area of your life — a place where you experienced a lack of "holding." Turn toward whatever issue you are struggling with and feel you need to work on. Set the intention to become closer and more intimate with the issue, so that you can begin to understand the truth of what's there. The goal is to let go of the need to "fix it," which itself is an expression of mistrust. The optimizing force or evolutionary impulse still exists, but it's buried inside the contraction and covered over by defensive mechanisms and compensatory ego strategies. By turning toward the issue, you can invite it to reveal what is really there.

Then, with your current state of maturity, you will be able to process whatever undigested pain remains. It's important to understand that the contraction was created when your nervous system was less developed and unable to process certain experiences. As an adult, you have more capacity to hold those traumatic imprints, so that the energy that is trapped within the contraction can naturally release itself.

We don't realize that much of what we have learned about processing and changing our behavior is rooted in mistrust — the exact mechanisms that reinforce the ego. By approaching our most difficult challenges in this way, basic trust is gradually restored. Moreover, we discover that being present, open, and in contact with the loss allows transformation to unfold and obstacles to dissolve naturally. There is a sense of innate guidance and dynamism that we can trust, as our instincts begin to relax and realign with our connection to existence.

Here's a four-step contemplative practice you can use to work through loss of trust:

(continued on next page)

Step 1. Choose an area of life in which you feel the lack of trust — an area where you exert effort and struggle and never seem to accept trust naturally.

Step 2. Once you've identified this area, close your eyes and let yourself feel your relationship to it. Feel whatever emotions are there: mistrust, fear, shame, anger, frustration, pain, sadness. Don't try to fix these emotions, just allow yourself to be open and authentically connect to this area of your life. Sense into your body and feel any stress associated with it: tension, exhaustion, strain, anger, shame, anxiety or whatever else might be there. As your presence infuses the contraction, you invite the evolutionary impulse or optimizing force to begin to flow again. Become more and more present. See if you can relax enough around the contraction to be curious about your own experience. Then contemplate the following questions:

- ⌘ What am I doing to try to "make it work"?
- ⌘ What do I believe about this area of my life?
- ⌘ What do I tell myself about why I have to work so hard in this area?

Answering these questions will help you to understand who you are and how the ego operates in this particular situation.

Step 3. Now think back to your childhood. Can you sense what might have been missing in the holding environment that caused you to stop trusting and feel as if you had to take charge? Consider whether you received enough support, attunement, protection, resources, safety, guidance, nourishment, competence, empathy, attention, and love. When any of these basic trust needs are lacking, we often recreate the lack of holding that we experienced as children and perpetuate it in our lives.

Step 4. Consider what might happen if you began to relate to this particular area of life with openness, interest, and a willingness to discover how the optimizing force wants to move in this situation. By being in contact with the lost trust, you make room for the optimizing force to come alive again and begin to work in the situation, to function in and through you. ೞ

EXERCISE 2:
Restoring Basic Trust — A Partner Practice

One of the ways to recover basic trust with a partner is to focus on an incident that created a break in trust. Use the Mutual Awakening Practice that I shared in Chapter Three, as soon as you experience the pain of mistrust. When you use this process, it's especially important that you retain the attitude of openness and curiosity about the truth of what is there. If you start to take on the desire to "solve" the problem you will automatically move into realm of the ego.

Step 1. Each of you answer the question: *What am I experiencing?* Don't react to each other at this stage. Simply listen as your partner describes the pain they are experiencing at the loss of trust.

Step 2. Then close your eyes and each of you answer the question: *What are we experiencing?* Loop back and forth and take your time to feel the common loss.

Step 3. As your shared consciousness is turned toward the mistrust that may have developed, the optimizing force will reveal what is needed, energy will be released, and further understanding will continue to arise if you stay open. So repeat the process and answer the question again: *What are we experiencing?* ◌

EXERCISE 3:
Basic Trust — Creating a Holding Environment

Another way to restore basic trust is to become aware of your relationship to the "holding" in your current environment. Often, we unconsciously recreate the same lack we experienced in childhood. You may want to use a journal for this practice.

Step 1. Ask yourself the following general question first:

⌘ Do I have what I need now so that I can relax and participate in the unfolding of my life and the manifestation of my highest potentials?

Step 2. Consider your physical environment and ask yourself the following:

⌘ Is anything missing?

⌘ Do I need more comfort, beauty, order, or stimulation?

⌘ Do I feel safe and protected?

⌘ Do I have enough space and resources?

Step 3. Now, consider your relationships and ask yourself:

⌘ Do I need more support, stimulation, love, acceptance, depth, challenge, or joy?

⌘ What could I do to provide these things in a relaxed, self-supportive way?

Step 4. Continue to look at other areas of your life, and ask yourself questions about your health, your finances, your work, and your creativity. When you recognize that you need something, allow yourself to have it if possible. This will build a growing trust in yourself and in your life. ৪

EXERCISE 4:
Living Daylight Meditation

This meditative practice can be used to reconnect with that original, undifferentiated, boundless consciousness of pure love that A.H. Almaas called the "living daylight." As a baby, your natural connection with that consciousness was the source of basic trust. Reconnecting with the living daylight through regular meditation is a powerful way to rebuild basic trust.

As with all the meditative practices in this book, I suggest you read through these instructions a few times until you are familiar with the process, and then put the book aside, find a place that's comfortable, and do the practice. If you would like to do this practice with guidance, you can download a free audio version of the Living Daylight Meditation at: www.EvolutonaryCollective.com.

Step 1. Sit still and close your eyes. Allow yourself to relax and take a few deep breaths. Turn your focus and attention inward.

Step 2. Consciously let everything be as it is and simply observe everything that you might be concerned about: your work, the people in your life, your health, all of it. Let everything simply be as it is. You don't have to get rid of anything. Allow your concerns to be there and relax around them. Imagine your worries are a bunch of dogs that you are walking, each of them on a leash. When the dogs relax, the leashes relax. You are still holding them, but they're not taut in your hands. Nor are they pulling you away from being present.

Step 3. Invite yourself to relax deeply. Your body knows how to do this. It knows exactly how to let go and remain alert at the same time. Your muscles, your nerves, even your bones know how to release tension. Now imagine that you are immersed in a dimension of beautiful, soft, golden light. The light has descended into your room and it's penetrating into your body through the top of your head. Allow the light to come inside you, allow it to relax your mind and penetrate the traffic of your thoughts. Then allow the light to penetrate even

(continued on next page)

deeper into your heart, relaxing any structures of defensiveness or fragility. Feel your heart softening and the light filling every part of your being.

Step 4. Now feel the light restoring your awareness and clearing the consciousness of your mind. Allow your head, your mind to awaken, as it is bathed in this light. Allow the light to continue to penetrate and grow stronger within you. Feel your connectivity to the light, the universe, and divine intelligence. Feel the parts of you that usually are like closed loops open up and become channels for knowledge and intelligence that is coming from a much higher vibration. Continue to breathe deeply and relax, bathed in the living daylight, within and without.   ⁐

EXERCISE 5:
Exploring Relative Trust

In this exercise, take the time to focus on the foundation of trust in a particular relationship that you care about deeply.

Step 1. Look at the degree of trust that exists currently. Ask yourself these questions:

- What allows me to trust this person?
- What allows the other person to trust me?
- In what ways do I trust myself in this relationship?
- In what ways do I not trust myself?
- What inspires confidence in this relationship?

(continued on next page)

Step 2. If you don't trust the other person or yourself, think about each of the qualities we've been exploring and ask yourself:

- ⌘ Is the mistrust stemming from a lack of integrity?
- ⌘ Is pride getting in the way?
- ⌘ Is mistrust stemming from a lack of clarity or a misalignment of expectations?
- ⌘ Is it because of my intentions or those of the other person?
- ⌘ Do I have the same vision for the relationship?
- ⌘ Is it a result of a lack of capacity?
- ⌘ Is mistrust occurring due to a lack of tangible results or effectiveness in following through?

Step 3. Once you determine exactly what is missing, see what may be done to strengthen and restore trust. For example, if you don't trust your partner because he or she lacks the capability to communicate clearly and with sensitivity, could you discuss the situation to see if your partner is willing to receive some coaching to improve communication and thereby improve your relationship? Or if you don't trust yourself because you realize you expect too much from your partner — *more than they expect from you* — maybe you can sit down together and share your concerns honestly. Each of you can state your expectations, become more conscious, and tell each other if you're uncomfortable with those expectations. Sometimes, the mere act of acknowledging together what is missing and determining how to bring it into existence in your relationship restores trust. ✂

For supplementary content, including audios, videos, and exercises, visit: www.EvolutionaryRelationshipsBook.com/bonus

Notes

1   Stephen M. R. Covey, *The Speed of Trust: The One Thing that Changes Everything*, New York, NY: Free Press, 2005.

2   A.H. Almaas, *Facets of Unity: The Enneagram of Holy Ideas*, Boulder, CO: Shambhala Publications, 2000.

3   Ibid.

4   Ibid.

5   Ibid.

CHAPTER EIGHT
The Fifth Principle: Openness

Only someone who is ready for everything, who doesn't exclude
any experience, even the most incomprehensible,
will live the relationship with another person as something alive
and will himself sound the depths of his own being.

~ Rainer Maria Rilke, *Letters to a Young Poet*

When I close my eyes, I can see my mother's smile. Standing on the porch with her hands on her hips, her smile would reach all the way into her warm hazel-green eyes, as she watched my spinning five-year-old body cartwheeling across the well-manicured lawn. My mother's love was palpable — a nourishing, sustaining presence, pervasive and assumed, like the sunlight and the air. I can picture her stepping out from under the porch into the sunlight, her wavy hair falling over her face as she leaned down for me to run into her arms. She would spin me around and then carry me inside for lunch. She was unselfconsciously beautiful, her attention focused on the beauty of everyone else.

As a child, I didn't think much about what made her so inviting and what created the ease I felt in being close to her. Openness, like trust, is one of those qualities that is invisible and effortless when it's present. As I moved into adulthood and learned how rare it is to encounter a truly open person whose heart and mind are relaxed and welcoming, I came to value more deeply the gift my mother gave me.

She was by no means perfect, but she was reliably open, available, and understanding. She also was willing to be real, authentic, and uncomplicated about it, and she invited me to be open as well. I never felt that I needed to maneuver, strategize, or manipulate in order to reach her or get her attention. If I did something that disappointed her, I could feel how it affected her directly. She didn't seem to add any extra emotional drama to the experience; she simply provided accurate human feedback, which is a rare and precious tool when it comes to navigating relationships. If I did something that made her proud or delighted, she was equally easy to find. She didn't withhold her feelings and natural responses, but allowed them to flow freely and transparently. I could feel her as she felt me, and this openness and vulnerability continued to characterize our relationship until the end of her life and even through the process of her death.

Openness is another essential Activating Principle of Evolutionary Relationships. Openness is a state of being available to all possibilities. When we are open, we welcome whatever arises, with an interest to be present and encounter it fully. We are ready to see and experience ourselves, each other, and whatever exists in the moment as it is. We also are open to the situation remaining as it is or changing, since openness creates the space for transformation. As a result, openness is a state of fluidity and presence that is unmarred by fixations, rigidity, preferences, judgments, positions, assumptions, and preconceptions.

In the previous chapter, we explored the principle of trust, and the way in which trust allows us to recover our original relationship to reality. In the same way, openness and its closely connected state of vulnerability allow us to recover our relationship with the true nature of our essential self and our soul's origination point.

Openness is the Nature of the Soul

Openness is one of the main ways we come into direct contact with our soul. The soul is by nature open: it is impressionable, spacious, light, receptive, and available to all possibilities and potentials. The soul also is porous to the "Great Mystery" — a term often used by indigenous cultures to describe the nature of being and of God. This mystery becomes accessible when we are fully open, and its potentials are limitless.

Openness allows us to sense the causal dimension of existence and the more ethereal aspects that never may be fully known. Yet, the "Great Mystery" infuses everything, is within our reach, and can become part of our consciousness ... when we open to it.

Our ability to remain connected to our soul depends largely upon the presence of basic trust, which we explored in the last chapter. For most people, when basic trust recedes, our ability to stay in touch with the openness and vulnerability of our soul is lost. When we restore our faith that existence is innately good and nurturing, we relax and open our heart and mind to the possibility of whatever arises. We no longer feel the need to protect ourself behind the closed doors of rigid thinking, fixed ideas, and limiting beliefs. We are available and in contact with our essential self.

The human soul is uniquely impressionable and malleable. By design, it is open to learning and influence. More than any other creature on Earth, humans' intense degree of impressionability makes it possible for us to be conditioned, to grow, and to develop. Most animals, insects, birds, and reptiles have pre-programmed instincts that limit the scope of their potential. Human beings clearly have hardwired instincts too, but we also have an enormous range of possibility due to our conscious and subconscious impressionability. Our receptivity allows us to receive new information, take it in, and respond, learn, and grow as a result.

We feel the soul's impressionability when we learn to pay attention to it. Think about the consciousness of a baby: it is smooth, fluid, and tender. At this early stage when the baby has not yet developed fixed ways of being, the true nature of the soul is closer to the surface and more palpable.

Starting with infancy, impressions are made on our soul through either repetitive or intense experiences which produce set patterns that shape who we are and how we respond to the world. For example, if we are lovingly cared for with an appropriate amount of attention to who we really are, and if our uniqueness is recognized and supported, we likely will feel self-confident and maintain an attuned sense of self. However, if we are consistently treated with neglect and disrespect, we may grow up feeling unworthy and become self-deprecating.

When our conditioning is misaligned with who we are, the impressions in our soul will become fixed and rigid structures that limit us and keep us in repetitive patterns. We then will feel stuck, contracted, and alienated from our depths. The more we felt threatened, abandoned, or insecure as babies and young children, the more likely it is that our ego structure will develop in ways that encase us in thick, defensive walls of fixed ideas, images and rigid beliefs. Ego structures are designed to filter our experience — to let some experiences in and keep others out. That's why human beings tend to have selective memory and perception.

It is important to realize that some souls, if attacked and physically abused even once, will suffer damage that causes lasting effects. If we've been conditioned in a dominating environment though excessive control and negative feedback, most of us will become defensive and closed. Then, openness and vulnerability will seem dangerous and unwise, and we will be too afraid to be shaped by outside influences. We won't allow ourselves to be influenced by other people or situations because we will fear being made into something against our will. If we examine the way most people function, we see that defensiveness commonly is considered to be normal and intelligent adult behavior. Consequently, many of us are overly careful not to intrude on others, nor do we want other people intruding on us. We sense the soul's vulnerability and we protect it.

On the other hand, if our early development happens in supportive and nurturing conditions, we will remain naturally open. We will be able to learn and grow in a way that doesn't limit or block our impressionability.

Remaining open depends on our holding environment, since it primarily determines whether our full range of potentials will continue to be available to us and whether our growth will continue to dynamically unfold. Ideally, our family of origin provides experiences that allow us to feel free, fluid and flexible, and which permit our creativity to be fully activated.

The soul's impressionability also is reflected in our physical makeup. Neuroscientists continue to be amazed by what they are discovering about the plasticity of the brain — its capacity to change and develop in response to outside influences, not just in early childhood but throughout our lifespan.

> *Experience can create structural changes in the brain. … Neuroplastic changes not only reveal structural alterations, but they are accompanied by changes in brain function, mental experience (such as feelings and emotional balance), and bodily states (such as response to stress and immune function).*[1]

When you embark on an Evolutionary Relationship and commit to being fully available for the deepest potentials to unfold, you and your partner probably will encounter subtle layers of defensiveness. Pay close attention to what you are experiencing, since you'll likely bump into these psychic structures, barriers that keep your soul closed off. Some spiritual healers who have highly developed perceptual capacities claim to see these structures. They describe them as taking certain shapes or being made of different substances: some appear hard, like steel, rock, or wood; some are thick and dense, like rubber or clay; others are raw, like an open wound; and some feel numb, like scar tissue. As your subtle capacities develop through practicing together, you will be able to sense these deeper layers too.

One way to identify psychic defense structures that are hampering an Evolutionary Relationship is to discern their particular qualities. Focus on an area of the relationship where you feel closed and somewhat disconnected. Try to approach the blockage not as a psychological concept but as if it were a physical substance or structure. Close your eyes and use your inner senses to feel into what is there. For example, if you experience yourself as being numb, attempt to perceive the exact quality of the disconnection or lack of sensation. Can you see an image of the structure? If you get close to it, what is it made of? Is it dense, thick, light, still, moving, hot, cold?

What other physical qualities are present? Does the structure manifest as a certain taste, or smell, or sound?

As we discussed in the previous chapter, the first and most important step toward softening egoic constructs is simply to be present and get as close to them as you can. Imagine going inside the structure. What do you feel? Does it seem safe or suffocating? Is it tight or spacious? As you bring your awareness to the defensive structure that is displacing your natural openness, you'll find it beginning to reveal itself to you and starting to change. Remember to just be close to it and remain engaged, rather than focusing on trying to fix or change the egoic structure. Also realize that some degree of ego development is necessary and inescapable to help us grow and mature. It only becomes problematic when the ego overdevelops in order to compensate for what is lacking in the holding environment.

Openness is the natural, original state of our souls. When that openness has been compromised through early life trauma, our spiritual work will need to focus on the places where we are contracted and defensive. By turning our full consciousness toward these places, the pain or intensity that we were unable to process as children can begin to unwind. When this happens, we experience "opening" as bursts of spontaneous understanding and revelations, because our energies are liberated as our patterns dissolve. Freedom and flexibility return and potentials and possibilities are present again. This openness activates the evolutionary impulse by making space for it to express its natural tendency, which is to free us and transform our experience toward greater and greater truth, creativity, and love. By paying attention to openness and vulnerability, we turn in the direction of recovering our fundamental connection to our own essential essence, and with it, we activate our capacity for mutuality.

Mutual Openness

Openness is more easily noticed in relationship and more difficult to access alone. When we bring openness and vulnerability into our relationship, we allow what is natural to unfold between us. Openness means that we are available to an infinite number of possibilities. In an Evolutionary Relationship, it means that we can begin to work at higher and higher levels. Together, we can learn to disidentify with our normal, limited ways of knowing ourselves and open ourselves up to mystical and mutual dimensions of experience.

The first step in mutually engaging with openness is simply to focus your attention on what it is, since it's invisible to our everyday awareness. When we share openness with someone, it can feel so natural, so simple, and so effortless that it easily can be missed. Openness translates into rapport, understanding, spontaneity, flow, and often joy and love. Without it, communication becomes difficult, trust erodes, and difficulties quickly seem insurmountable. Becoming mutually conscious of what it means to be open can focus and channel the power of this principle into an evolutionary catalyst.

Mutual openness, as an Activating Principle of evolutionary relating, is the ability to be vulnerable and transparent with each other and whatever the moment is presenting. It's the willingness to let go of agendas and attempts to "get someplace," and the ability to allow whatever wants to unfold and deepen. As experienced meditators learn, when you let go and let things be as they are, something mystical takes over. The same principle applies in conscious relating. When you approach each other and the relationship with openness, curiosity and acceptance, a deep enjoyment and sharing occurs. You discover that you love to explore greater mysteries together. As you learn to share with each other at this level, you will rediscover the true nature of the soul: It delights in Great Mystery touching reality and being known.

Five Keys to Accessing Openness

Here are some simple tips on how to mutually access openness:

Key 1: Become aware of expectations, fixed positions, and preconceived ideas about yourself, your partner, or the relationship.

Key 2: Be willing to explore these fixed concepts and, if possible, let them go.

Key 3: Investigate any sense of contractedness or fear.

Key 4: Actively challenge self-images that you have developed (e.g.: "I am this kind of person" or "I am that kind of person").

Key 5: Become attuned to the movement of the optimizing force, follow its dynamism, and stop trying to fix or stabilize reality.

As you pay attention to becoming more open together, freshness, innocence, and playfulness will return. If you always are trying to fix problems or get somewhere, your shared experience can become heavy and stale.

I'm not suggesting that problems should be avoided or allowed to fester. Rather, I am encouraging you to use the techniques I've been sharing to mutually open yourselves and then be present with whatever arises. Simply holding uncomfortable feelings in an open-ended way, with curiosity and trust, is surprisingly powerful.

Openness and Vulnerability

Openness is intrinsically connected to vulnerability, and with relationships, vulnerability is the doorway to intimacy. Without vulnerability, our relationships are reduced to separate egos interacting with each other, bumping into each other. We experience ourselves and each other as objects, and there is no space of mutuality or interpenetration of consciousness through which the evolutionary impulse can move.

In our culture, we have been encouraged not to be vulnerable or sensitive to ourselves. As a result, we have been trained to minimize our real experience. Just look at the ways we push past our needs and limitations. In fact, being stoic and insensitive to our own reality is often glorified. We forget to eat, work past exhaustion, don't take care of ourselves, and ignore our feelings of being overwhelmed, hurt, shy, frightened, loving, attracted, excited.

Consequently, vulnerability is a state that many of us are afraid to experience. Too often, we associate it with being weak or defenseless. This is hardly surprising, since the root of vulnerability is the Latin word *vulnarare*, which means "to wound." Common definitions of the term include "susceptible to being wounded or hurt," "open to mortal attack," and "exposed to danger." In relationships, though, many of us do understand, at least in theory, that vulnerability is a positive quality. Yet, most of us find it difficult to soothe our instinctive fear of exposing ourselves.

Defensiveness is the opposite of vulnerability. If you are unwilling to increase your ability to be vulnerable and open, you likely display some of the following characteristics of defensiveness:

- A need to control
- Rigidity expressed through strong immovable beliefs, attitudes, opinions, tastes, and preferences
- Deadness, numbness, and a lack of compassion
- Isolation and withdrawal from life and other people
- Over-sensitivity

If any of these traits describe you or someone with whom you are in a relationship, consider the ways in which you or the other person deal with vulnerability. *How do you avoid being vulnerable? How does your partner avoid being vulnerable? What are the effects of this avoidance on each of you and on the relationship? What has displaced openness?* Don't judge yourself or your partner for a lack of vulnerability; just begin to explore how it operates in your life and in your relationship. And then, without trying to fix it, hold these questions: *What would it take for you to open up again? What would it take for your partner to do the same? What would it take to open up more than you ever have to anyone?* By exploring these questions, you probably will discover that courage and a willingness to engage more fully and take risks is necessary to improving your connection. Remember, the goal is to be mutually committed to being open together.

Fortunately, as we mature and spiritually develop, we learn that vulnerability does not imply weakness. To the contrary, we discover that

In an Evolutionary Relationship,
being vulnerable means having the strength
and maturity to accept the totality of our
experience and being open to the truth of
the moment in a real, authentic manner.

vulnerability brings openness, sensitivity, and a lack of defensiveness. In fact, it's an essential prerequisite for our continued evolution, because in order to move to higher levels of consciousness, we need to move through our conditioned, defensive responses and become open again to the influence and essence of the optimizing force.

Rather than being a source of weakness, vulnerability gives us strength. As researcher Brene Brown writes, "Vulnerability sounds like truth and feels like courage. Truth and courage aren't always comfortable, but they're never weakness."[2] Brown, who studied vulnerability intensively and gave a viral TEDx talk on the topic, defines vulnerability as "uncertainty, risk, and emotional exposure." Vulnerability is not inherently a good or bad emotion, she claims, but rather, "it is the core of all emotions and feelings. To feel is to be vulnerable." She has concluded from her research that the reason people reject vulnerability is that they tend to associate it with "dark emotions like fear, shame, grief, sadness, and disappointment." However, she writes, "what most of us fail to understand and what took me a decade of research to learn is that vulnerability is also the cradle of the emotions and experiences we crave. Vulnerability is the birthplace of love, belonging, joy, courage, empathy, and creativity."[3]

It's important to feel your vulnerability, while at the same time feeling your power and centeredness. It's not about being in control and in charge, but rather about balancing, including, and integrating your strength, your responsibility, and every other positive attribute within you and the other person. You can hold it all. Being vulnerable means expressing the fullness of our love, strength, joy, and creativity.

In an Evolutionary Relationship, the commitment you make to each other is to be as open as you can be at any given moment, regardless of whether what arises between you feels blissful and ecstatic, or uncomfortable and threatening. You also agree to give up the right to be defensive. That doesn't mean you won't experience defensiveness, but when you do, your commitment is to explore it together, in the moment. Withdrawing or trying to control whatever makes you uncomfortable is not an option at this level of relating.

Not Knowing and Openness to Mystery

So far, we've primarily been studying openness in relation to our ego blockages and defensive structures. However, as these mechanisms start to soften and release, we begin to experience the more exciting dimensions of openness — the capacity to embrace our unseen potentials and the Great Mystery itself.

In order to realize such higher potentials, the journey requires that we continue to discover and unfold our true essence. Only by letting go of fixed identities and partial realities may we discover that each of us is a unique expression flowing from the mystery of existence. Our capacities and potentials truly are infinite, because we are part of that mystery.

The key to accessing our higher potentials is the ability to assume a posture of *not knowing*. To understand what it truly means to *not know*, consider the following model:

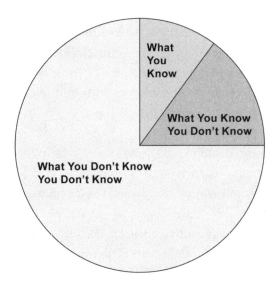

Imagine that the above circle represents everything that could possibly be known on every level of existence. Clearly, that totality can't exist inside any circle, but use your imagination. First, there is a small segment of possible knowledge that you know that you know, probably an incredibly small sliver. That is the "what you know" section of the diagram. Second, there's a segment that represents all the things "you know you don't know."

For example, I know that I don't know how to speak most languages. I also know that I don't know about fixing cars, brain surgery, nanotechnology, and what it will be like to die. Healthy curiosity leads most of us to inquire about what we don't know, through reading, studying, taking classes, and learning from others, since most of us want to expand our comprehension of the world.

The third and largest segment of the circle represents a body of knowledge about which you are totally unaware — you don't even know that you don't know about it! So when I refer to "not knowing," this is the part of the circle I'm pointing to, and it represents a different order of not knowing — a vast realm of what "you don't know you don't know." This segment includes the questions we don't even know to ask because it's a realm we don't even realize exists. Here is where the true mystery lives. Here is where infinite potentials reside. This realm of not knowing is waiting for you to pay attention and make yourself available to it.

Coming into contact with the mystery of existence requires the deepest of dives into openness. Mysticism is the realm of human endeavor devoted to connecting with hidden dimensions — the endless richness of the sacred and its myriad forms of expression. We never can fully know it, understand it, or experience it. Yet, as we open ourselves to not knowing and if we pay attention, we can begin to connect with the mystery of being ... and the mystery of being together.

As an Activating Principle of evolutionary relating, openness gives us the power to let go and turn toward the mystery with a relaxed curiosity. The mystical dimension comes into awareness when we come together not knowing who we are, who the other is, or what is possible between us. We dissolve into a profound receptivity that invites mystical revelation. When I was with Peter, we were taken into different worlds together, real and substantial worlds, filled with love and light. Other times, we would enter into a space together early in the morning that would carry us through the rest of the day. These experiences were magical and playful, and they had a mystical flavor, as if we were playing with God, delighting in existence, and creating new forms of pleasure and enjoyment.

Due to the precious time I had with Peter and the explorations I have made with other advanced souls, I have no doubt that mystical revelation and mystical experiences can be accessed through the Eight Activating

Principles. Through the portal of Evolutionary Relationships, we truly can enter into "Heaven." Mystical experiences always are a great blessing, even when we encounter them alone. But when we step into the mystery together and realize that we are experiencing the hidden realities that gave birth to this world, the immensity of grace elicits overflowing gratitude. My personal experience of entering into these realms, first with Peter and now with members of our Evolutionary Collective, always is exquisite and ever-new. By being together in the ultimate state of openness and surrender, we move into unity consciousness and new potentials are released.

As we jointly surrender to this profound level of openness, we experience a mutual transfiguration: Our consciousness expands and our minds, hearts, and bodies are infused with new light and love. Mystical experiences are ineffable, impossible to explain clearly, so they often are expressed in poetic fashion. Ultimately, though, words merely point to sensations that can only be felt by being in the experience directly.

> *The joy of a mutual mystical experience is that even when there are no words for it, both partners know they have shared it and that it is real.*

Openness is the portal through which we mutually enter new dimensions, and "not knowing" is the posture that allows us to move deeply into extraordinary new possibilities. In order to discover higher potentials of mutual awakening, we need to encounter reality directly and release preconceived ideas of what is there. The moment we conclude that we "already know," we close down the portal to what is possible together. In Evolutionary Relationships, we must relish fleeting discoveries of what is actually there, who we are, and what potentials the space between us holds. Openness allows us to access the very edge of the evolutionary impulse, which is a crucial aspect of mutual awakening and the start of the WEvolution.

The Fruit of Openness: Spontaneity

When we practice being open, vulnerable and not knowing together, the field between us opens up and reveals the rich possibilities of human interaction. As this happens, we experience the fruit of openness — the possibility of being free and utterly spontaneous together.

Openness in relationship shows up as a lack of self-consciousness. We find our innocence again, and we abandon our strategies and coping mechanisms. We stop premeditating, holding back, pretending, hiding, and being self-protective. We let go and relinquish control. There no longer is anything or anyone to block the free expression of who we are and what is possible. In this state, we often feel like young children again: light, carefree, and playful.

The experience of shared openness leads to spontaneity, and it is pure delight. Spontaneity can be expressed in being wildly creative together, brilliant, loving, or silly. There's nothing as joyful as spontaneous interaction, because it is a channel for the expression of our authentic selves. We forget all about our ego's habitual worrying about how we appear, and we trust that we'll be able to handle whatever comes up. We let go of self-control, and freely enjoy and celebrate our interaction. It's as though an inner sun comes out and lifts our spirits. Surprise, wonder, and unexpected revelations can emerge between us.

As your Evolutionary Relationship grows, the content of your experience may weave back and forth: Sometimes your focus will land on the simple presence of the moment; other times a contraction or difficulty will arise that seeks your attention; and yet other times new discoveries, love, creativity, or spiritual revelations will captivate you. Mutual openness means that no matter what arises, you must be courageous. What arises may be painful, uncomfortable, intense, or terrifying. It may overwhelm you and your partner with joy and with more love than you've ever imagined. It may shatter your old reality or dissolve who you thought you were. No matter what arises, if you stay open together and pay attention to what is present in the moment, the optimizing force will continue to flow and move you forward. When you fling open the doors of your soul, there is no limit to what can unfold through you and between you.

EXERCISE:
Exploring Your Relationship to Openness

Step 1. In quiet contemplation or in a journal, think about and then answer the following questions:

- ⌘ Is there a way in which I am not open in a particular relationship? Think of an example.
- ⌘ How does the lack of openness occur?
- ⌘ What do I do (or not do) that expresses itself as contraction or defensiveness?
- ⌘ How do I experience not being open and how does it feel?
- ⌘ Who am I being when I am not open?
- ⌘ How might my partner describe me when I'm not being open?

Step 2. Now ask yourself:

- ⌘ Am I willing to be open and discover what actually exists in my relationship and what is possible?
- ⌘ Am I ready to allow the relationship to move and unfold naturally? ✂

For supplementary content, including audios, videos, and exercises, visit: www.EvolutionaryRelationshipsBook.com/bonus

Notes

1   Dan Siegel, *The Mindful Brain: Reflection and Attunement in the Cultivation of Well-Being*, New York, NY: W.W. Norton & Company, 2007.

2   Brene Brown, *Daring Greatly: How the Courage to Be Vulnerable Transforms the Way We Live, Love, Parent, and Lead*, New York, NY: Gotham Books, 2012, p. 37.

3   Ibid, pp. 34-35.

CHAPTER NINE
The Sixth Principle: Essential Uniqueness

[T]he ultimate touchstone of friendship is not improvement,
neither of the other nor of the self,
the ultimate touchstone is witness, the
privilege of having been seen by someone and the equal
privilege of being granted the sight of the essence of another....

~ David Whyte, *Consolations*

When you watch a great artist perform — a musician or a dancer, for example — what is it that captivates you? It's not simply technical excellence, beauty, precision, or virtuosity, although all of these play a part in their brilliance. There's something else that holds your attention fixed, some particular quality that is unique to that individual and their expression. You could listen to a hundred violinists play the same piece of music, and each would have a slightly different quality. The notes and the melody might be the same, but each individual musician brings some essential character to the expression that is theirs and theirs alone.

Those who achieve greatness don't stop at simply developing their craft and emulating other people's styles. They do the hard work of discovering their own authentic sound or voice, that form of expression that touches the depth of truth within themselves. They fight what poet E.E. Cummings described as "the hardest battle which any human being can fight … to be nobody-but-yourself in a world which is doing its best, night and day, to make you everybody else."[1]

Martha Graham, the woman considered to be the "mother of modern dance" put this into words when speaking to her lifelong friend, Agnes De Mille: "There is a vitality, a life force, an energy, a quickening that is translated through you into action, and because there is only one of you in all of time, this expression is unique."[2]

The uniqueness that Graham was describing is one of the key Activating Principles in Evolutionary Relationships. I use the term "essential uniqueness" because it's not surface individuality that I want us to consider — all the relative differences in appearance, expression, and personality that create the wonderfully varied kaleidoscope of humanity. Rather, what I'm pointing to is something more fundamental — the intrinsic substance of who we are as the essential self.

My experience of essential uniqueness is that I am in touch with the purest, most refined, most intimate sense of who I am. It's the irreducible "Patricia" that exists through all the changing circumstances of my life, and its core, its flavor, is sustained and nurtured as I develop and am able to express it more fully. As people age, they often comment on how their sense of self internally doesn't match their experience when they look in the mirror. This incongruity points to a deeper, subjective sense of self that is distinct but somehow elusive.

We each have an essence that is all our own, that is not replicated anywhere else in this vast cosmos. It is not something we invent, but something we can rediscover — the core essence or pattern of who we are. Our uniqueness is self-existent and doesn't need any outside evidence to reinforce its truth. I like to think of it as the particular spark of Divinity that is at the core of every being. When we meet another person in an Evolutionary Relationship, it is our essential, unique self that is connecting to the essential, unique self in the other. In the process of creating and sustaining an Evolutionary

Relationship, we each need to learn to live more completely from our own core essence and to recognize and honor the essence of the other.

Perspectives on Uniqueness

In religious and spiritual traditions, there are many different perspectives on the reality and qualities of this unique self, and it would take a whole book, if not many, to provide a comprehensive analysis of this subject matter. In general, most mystical paths point toward transcendence of the relative, limited ego-self, though not all of them distinguish between the ego and a deeper dimension of the personal self. Some approaches, like the Buddhist or Vedantic traditions, for example, put more emphasis on awakening to a sense of self that is universal, impersonal, and non-relative. However, there are other paths that put more emphasis on the development of the individual soul, and make a clear distinction between the ego and the personal soul or essential self.

One of the teachers I studied with, A.H. Almaas, was influenced by the Sufi tradition and placed a lot of emphasis on the personal dimension of "being," which he called "the personal essence" or sometimes "the pearl." He writes, "The pearl beyond price, the incomparable pearl, the personal aspect of Essence is central for many important reasons. It is actually the true essential personality. It is the person. It is experienced as oneself. When the individual finally perceives it, the contented expression often is 'but this is me!' The sense is of oneself as a precious being. There is then a fullness, a completeness, and a contentment."[3]

Almaas also makes the important distinction between the personal essence and the ego, pointing out that many psychologists confuse the two. "We must remember that the ego is a structure, or structured process, whereas the pearl is Essence, which means the pearl is an ontological Presence."[4] In my work with Evolutionary Relationships, I often refer to this unique, individual distinctness as the "origination point." It is a portal of expression or an opening from which our unique expression pours into all of existence, for all time. It is experienced as multidimensional, finite, and eternal.

In other words, our personal essence is a quality of being that we are born with, whereas the ego is an image that has been created over time in reaction to others and the world. As we have explored in earlier chapters, the development of the ego is based on identifying with a self-image or a conglomerate of self-images, none of which are self-existent. The self-images are filters through which we perceive ourselves. We reinforce these filters through the ways we think and talk about ourselves, and how we experience the world.

The ego is innately fragile and needs continual shoring up and mirroring. Our personal essence, on the other hand, is unique and distinct and has the capacity to be itself without any outside reinforcement or self-reflection. When we are in touch with our personal essence, we have the capacity to be ourselves even when the world doesn't see us or when we struggle to bring something into existence with little support. We witness this quality of essence in pioneers who move culture forward — people like Martha Graham or Martin Luther King, Jr., who remain true to themselves and the unique expression they bring into the world, even when the world pushes back or misinterprets them.

The American psychologist James Hillman beautifully wrote about the nature of uniqueness in his book *The Soul's Code.* Using the analogy of an acorn containing the imprint of the oak tree, he writes, "each person bears a uniqueness that asks to be lived and is already present before it can be lived."[5] Hillman borrows the term "daimon" from Plato and the Greeks to describe this unique pattern, but acknowledges that there have been many other terms in multiple languages that point to the same principle: "The concept of this individual soul-image has a long complicated history; its appearance in cultures is diverse and widespread and the names for it are legion." He points out that contemporary psychology and psychiatry have lost touch with this aspect of what it means to be human. "When it comes to accounting for the spark of uniqueness and the call that keeps us to it, psychology ... is stumped."[6] *The Soul's Code* is full of wonderful stories of great geniuses and world leaders that show how this inner spark calls the individual toward his or her destiny. But what Hillman is pointing to is not just seen in these rare and extraordinary individuals; it is an aspect of all of us.

Essential uniqueness is not about
particular talents or artistic gifts — it is
something everyone possesses.
If we are connected to our particular
spark of divinity, it will express itself
in whatever way is organic to our nature.

Essential uniqueness is about who we are, not what we do. The problem, however, is that we often are not in touch with our core nature. Generally, as we've discussed, we lose touch with it as we move through life and into a more superficial relationship with ourselves and others. Our relationships can either help us to remember our essential uniqueness, or they can do the opposite.

A story I love that illustrates this point comes from spiritual teacher Alan Cohen. In his book *The Wisdom of the Heart,* Cohen describes an African tribe in which the women, when pregnant, go out into the wilderness and pray until they "hear the song" of their unborn child. "They recognize that every soul has its own vibration that expresses its unique flavor and purpose," he writes. "When the women attune to the song, they sing it out loud. Then they return to the tribe and teach it to everyone else." He describes how this song then is sung at the child's birth and at every other key transition in his or her life. And he adds, "there is one other occasion upon which the villagers sing to the child. If at any time during his or her life, the person commits a crime or aberrant social act, the individual is called to the center of the village and the people in the community form a circle around them. Then they sing their song to them."[7]

What this story illustrates is that there are precious times when we all need to be reminded of who we really are. Moreover, when we act in ways that are incongruent with that essential spark of our divinity, our most important relationships are with those people who continue to relate to us as who we really are and who can "sing our song" to us.

What Is Your Spiritual Tincture?

Another term that points toward this dimension of experience is "tincture." The 17th Century theosophist Jakob Boehme used this term to express his sense of how the Divine has penetrated and permeated the living world. This term was introduced to me by the modern-day mystic Cynthia Bourgeault, who explains tincture as "essentially, a quality of aliveness. Everything alive has a tincture … a musk, fragrance, sparkle, uniquely its own and unmistakable. Tincture is a recognition of things by their inner spiritual scent."[8]

It may be easier, initially, to recognize this quality of essential uniqueness in someone else, particularly someone you have known and loved for a long time. If you think about the people you really love, you can get in touch with that unique, unmistakable sense of who they are, their inner soul that you would recognize even if they looked different physically. This is captured beautifully in the 2008 movie *The Curious Case of Benjamin Button*, where the titular character, played by Brad Pitt, ages in reverse before our eyes. During the movie, we see his essential self stay the same throughout the dramatic physical transformation. We also see the relationship he has with the woman who loves him shift and change as their ages differ or come closer, but fundamentally their connection remains the same.

You may have experienced a similar deep connection with someone you've not seen for many years, even decades. Although you both have aged and changed, some essential quality — their tincture — is instantly recognizable. As you move into the domain of evolutionary relatedness, your sensitivity to this quality will become stronger and stronger. You naturally will "tune in" to the particular tincture of new people as well and be aware of how these tinctures mingle and mix in the domain of relatedness.

A funny example of tincture recognition happened recently for Judy, one of the women working with me. I was teaching a class on essential uniqueness, and Judy had a powerful awakening to the particularity of herself and the other people in the room. Her comprehension remained strong that evening when she left the session and walked back to her hotel in New York. When she entered the lobby, there were dogs everywhere. Apparently, there was an international dog show nearby, and many of the contestants were staying at her hotel. Still alive with her revelations from our workshop, she said she experienced an intensification of how incredibly unique every dog was, and every owner. "I stood transfixed," she told me, "feeling all the differences, the particular tails, types of fur, tongues, and bodies. There was a sea of movement and sound: dogs with long legs, others with little stubby ones, eyes that were big and warm, and other eyes lost in fur. I simultaneously could feel the exquisite perfection in each dog being exactly the way they were."

Judy also noticed that this experience was different than just observing the scene "from the outside." She described it as happening "inside a new consciousness of feeling and knowing the brilliant and beautiful diversity in creation. My heart opened into a vaster connection to the love inherent in uniqueness." What she experienced in that moment is the kind of love we usually feel only for the people and animals we already know and cherish. However, when we are able to appreciate and touch the essential uniqueness of new people we meet, we truly have learned to access self-existent love — a love that resides at the core of who we are and who they are.

Peter's tincture still is very vivid for me. It had a particular flavor of depth and intensity, an essence that was light yet rich, while also nourishing, sensual, and peaceful. His tincture emanated an attracting force that I found irresistible — a strong, masculine presence of aliveness, teasing, taunting, demanding, but fully inviting and generous. The image that comes to mind is a male dancer who invites you to run to him so that he can lift you gracefully, gently, over his head and orient you to the heavens. Peter also possessed a rapturous beauty that was penetrating and mysterious. Interestingly, when he was still alive but not with me, I would feel his tincture, his particular "Peterness." It was uncanny — he could call me from afar (and vice versa), as we had a direct-dial line into each other's soul.

When Peter left my life, it was an abrupt, unexpected, and devastating event. He suffered a terrible car wreck and a debilitating brain injury, which left him bereft and me inconsolable. Tragically, I could feel his inner conflict and his connection to life fading. Eventually, Peter committed suicide, thereby releasing himself from a misery that went bone-deep. But even through the darkness that engulfed me after Peter's death, I realized that what we had found together would never be lost. Rather, a profound and sacred love continues to this day, despite his physical absence.

I quickly found that I still could tune into Peter's particular tincture and feel our eternal relationship. I deeply appreciate this quote from Cynthia Bourgeault: "'Eternal marriages' come into existence because they are part of the divine scheme. True love expresses the sacred promise that love is stronger than death."[9] I'm sure many of you have experienced this truth as well — that love continues beyond death. Later, I discovered that I could activate this field with others in my teaching work, if they too were willing to connect to one another from center-to-center, essence-to-essence.

Not only does our divine spark exist after death, I am convinced it exists before birth. A few months before I became pregnant — while I still was debating whether or not to have a child — I began to feel my child's essence hovering close to me. There was a distinct sense of someone being present, waiting for me to realize that we were meant to know each other and share this life together.

During my pregnancy, my son's quality became even more distinct. I would lie on the couch in our downtown loft in New York City in the late afternoons with my hands on my belly and feel his presence. Even then, before Alexander was born, I came to know and love him. And when he was placed into my arms after an exhausting birth, I immediately recognized him. I felt that same unique quality — holding this tiny eight-pound human being — that I felt when I met Peter for the first time. And decades later, Alexander's primordial essence hasn't changed, even though he's grown and developed in so many ways. His unique "Alex-ness" exists for me on a soul level.

The gift of a human life provides the opportunity to mature beyond ego-identification and develop a deeper, fuller sense of self and to follow its expression into the world and into relatedness. We tend to pay too much attention to what we think other people want us to be (i.e., what they will love and accept from us), rather than discovering this deeper source of power, creativity, and wisdom that abides within ourselves. Often, we hear success stories about people who finally gave up trying to conform to what the world and other people tell them to be, and who follow an innate sense of their own expression instead, regardless of whether the world can relate to it. This is the point when people contribute to the world in some unique way. These are the great musicians and artists who, after struggling to find their voice, their music, and their message, break through in a miraculous fashion. Instinctively, we know the difference between the authentic expression of a person's essence and a contrived attempt to produce a certain result.

It's not easy, in this world, to allow our essential uniqueness to flower. We are surrounded by messages dictating how we are supposed to be, who we are supposed to love, what we are supposed to feel, care about, think, believe, and so on. As babies, given our sensitivity and impressionability, we easily may become conditioned to that which undermines our essential uniqueness. Responding to our social environment is beneficial to some degree, but too much may be lost in the process.

Imagine as parents if we were awake to this aspect of essential uniqueness and were excited to discover and fully support exactly who our children are, instead of trying to shape them to match our ideals or who we need them to be for us. As the great Jewish mystic Martin Buber wrote, "Every man's foremost task is the actualization of his unique, unprecedented and never-recurring potentialities, and not the repetition of something that another, and be it even the greatest, has already achieved."[10]

Uniqueness in Relationship

Why is essential uniqueness so important for activating higher states of relatedness? To put it simply, it is the only place within ourselves from which an Evolutionary Relationship can occur. Ironically, if we go deeper than our personal essence and try to access more impersonal or universal dimensions of being, there is no "relating," because the nature of that dimension is unity or nonduality. When there are "not two" there is no relationship, only unity beyond all distinctions. Conversely, if we remain at surface-level relatedness, in which the self relates as the ego, an Evolutionary Relationship cannot emerge either, because then we remain two separate objects viewing the world through our filters and unable to make any contact. Real intimacy is threatening to the ego, which relies on its false sense of separateness to support its existence. It cannot afford to engage in actual connectivity because it will disappear. Therefore, it blocks deep relatedness to survive.

Evolutionary Relationships emerge only
when we connect soul-to-soul.
Such a connection resides neither in duality
nor nonduality, but in a space in-between
that encompasses both dimensions and
allows our unique essence to flourish.

As we enter into an Evolutionary Relationship, we are inviting uniqueness to become more central in our lives and in our relationships. By giving it a place to engage, our uniqueness develops and begins to shine. Pierre Teilhard de Chardin understood this when he wrote, "Love is the free and imaginative outpouring of the spirit over all unexplored paths. It links those who love in bonds that unite but do not confound, causing them to discover in their mutual contact an exaltation capable, incomparably more than any arrogance of solitude, of arousing in the heart of their being all that they possess of uniqueness and creative power."[11] Elsewhere, he wrote, "The special effect of love is to plunge the beings it draws together more deeply into themselves."[12]

The kind of love we share as we see each other deeply allows the ego to relax its grip. Together, we recover a sense of ourselves that feels simple, natural and free, and oftentimes, absolutely intoxicating. To gradually be returned to ourselves through the experience of relatedness, and to discover the uniqueness, originality, and freshness of who we are in every aspect of our lives, constitutes the hard and glorious work of why we are here.

Discovering Essential Autonomy

It's one thing to get in touch with your essential self; it's another thing altogether to live from it and abide in your essence as you relate with others. To be rooted in your origination point requires a kind of autonomy that is relatively rare. It also requires a conscious development beyond ego that most people have not acquired.

In our culture, we tend to associate autonomy with the ability to be independent and self-reliant. The root of autonomy combines the Greek words for "self" and "law," giving rise to its common meaning of "self-government," whether applied to an individual or a nation. Autonomy, in this sense, is related to the stage of development that Robert Kegan calls "self-authoring." It points to a capacity for independent thought and action, the ability to be guided by one's own values, judgments, and choices, rather than being swayed by social pressures or other people's agendas.

As we become interested in the potential of an Evolutionary Relationship, we need to discover this deeper kind of autonomy. As we've discussed, if we are too attached to our own independence and individual freedom, we will be unable to allow other people to touch us deeply. Consequently, conventional autonomy is an obstacle to mutual awakening. However, there is another level of autonomy — what I call "essential autonomy" — that does not conflict with relatedness at all. In fact, it enhances the experience of relatedness because it is the experience of each individual rooted in his or her own uniqueness. Evolutionary Relationships cannot truly flourish without it.

This deeper, essential autonomy is no longer about being independent of other people. Rather, it's about independence from our self-images, history, self-reflection, cultural conditioning, memories, and ways of objectifying ourselves and the world. Autonomy, in this sense, is the experience of direct contact with our essential self. When we become truly autonomous, it feels natural, transparent, and unselfconscious. It's like love or joy — we know it directly and it's not something we need to think about. The ego only knows itself through self-reflection or from the mirroring of others. However, contact with our essential self is definite and immediate. There's a sense of being "real" — like the difference between Pinocchio's wooden existence and his transformation into a "real boy." This sense of self is vivid, substantial, and alive.

Discovering and developing our true autonomy is a process that is enhanced by participating in an Evolutionary Relationship. Every time you and your partner do the Mutual Awakening Practice set forth in Chapter Three, you directly engage this sense of self. After a while, both of you will be able to taste the difference between the "wooden" Pinocchio — the sense of being separate and inside the filters of the ego — and being "real," which provides direct contact with your unique selves. The difference in experiencing this kind of immediacy and intimacy is palpable.

> *Our uniqueness is precious*
> *and valuable, and when we are able*
> *to disentangle it from our egos,*
> *our essence emerges as the*
> *sacred expression of our humanity.*

When we're in contact with our personal essence, we experience fulfillment, happiness and contentment, while also being wholly concerned for others. We live our lives unselfconsciously and we naturally devote our attention to other human beings and the world. There is no self-sacrifice or renunciation in this. Rather, we find living in this way deeply fulfilling, and it organically seems to provide us with the energy and enthusiasm to be of service. We also happen upon this world-centric perspective unintentionally. By being who we are and having the courage to live from our particular essential nature, we are exactly the gift that is needed. To me, it's logical that each of us is designed perfectly, in harmony with each other and the world, and that our distinctness is needed and wanted. The natural world seems to be created in this fashion, so it makes sense that we would be as well.

Essential autonomy also means we are open to learning and being influenced by other people in a way that enhances our genuine sense of self. As we open and habitual patterns dissolve, this quality of autonomy arises naturally, and we find ourselves thinking: *This is who I really am!* Our maturity becomes palpable to others and the expression of our potential satisfies our longings. When we are living from our ego, on the other hand, even if we are successful, we don't really feel fulfilled, at least not in the same way that true self-expression leaves us feeling. From essential autonomy, we see how to have the life we truly want, a life that reflects our depth and our real capacities, in which we can grow, contribute, and continue to develop. We simply are *being*, and this source of being originates from within us.

Clearly, essential autonomy is based on our uniqueness. As we turn toward each other with the intention of creating an Evolutionary Relationship and use the Mutual Awakening Practice, we discover each other's uniqueness. This practice is an invitation to see and feel each other at the core and realize that autonomy and a deep communion are one. As we welcome each other's depth and invite each other to show up fully as ourselves, the relatedness will continue to expand and reveal new possibilities. It's amazing to discover that we can be clear and distinct and yet have no boundaries separating us. Somehow our uniqueness, which is self-existent, doesn't need the usual, conventional boundaries to stay psychologically healthy. By being ourselves from the core, we project a strong, clear base from which to live and love. It's a relief to be free from the usual negotiations and compromises that typically keep us separate and unable to truly connect.

While in this deeper autonomy, it is important to understand that you will be open to influence, as you learn from and become more affected by others. Yet, you won't lose touch with the immediacy and distinctness of your own being. Your capacity for influence — both being open to it and being able to affect someone else — is a tremendously important and crucial element of the process of mutual awakening.

We will explore mutual influence more deeply in Chapter Ten, as we attempt to unlearn the habitual mistrust of others that society has taught us. The goal is to allow our essential autonomy the opportunity to feel various influences with more subtlety and discrimination while also sensing what is congruent with our own essence (i.e., what is aligned and what is not). It's like digesting food that is good for our body and expelling the rest. We want to integrate those aspects of influence that enhance and support who we are and why we are here.

When we identify with our self-image and more ego-driven forms of autonomy, we often feel that we need to hold ourselves separate and not expose ourselves to the influence of others. This is to be expected, since the ego was created through physical and emotional distancing. In order to individuate as young children, we needed to progressively become more and more independent from our mothers or caregivers. It was important to learn not to rely too much on other people or our environment. Becoming independent and separate at this stage in life is an important achievement. But later, this can manifest as an insistence on being alone, a refusal to listen to others, or a resistance to learning from teachers or those who might influence us.

Of course, at times it is important and can be useful to withdraw from the world and its constant stimuli in order to be quiet and listen more deeply to ourselves. We sometimes feel more freedom when no one else is around. Yet, a deeper freedom is found when we dis-identify with our self-images, when we disentangle ourselves from who we have learned to be, and when we experience connecting with our core essence. As this true freedom grows, we no longer need to separate from others and their influence; we can be fully available, fully connected, and still be ourselves.

The truth is that we never really seek separation. What we yearn for is to be ourselves. As youth, we separated to find ourselves: to discover who we are, to get in touch with what we want and what we like and care about, to discover how we really feel, what we think, and how we uniquely express ourselves and our potentials. But in order to establish Evolutionary Relationships, we must evolve beyond ingrained notions of independence and early individuation. Only then may we discover the deeper essential autonomy that will move our lives and relationships to a new level of love and possibility.

When you do the Mutual Awakening Practice, let go of your sense of identity and who you think you are. Try to discover exactly what is there on the edge of your experience in this moment. I've often said, don't even worry about "being human," which may sound a little strange, but it helps people let go of their automatic sense of identity. As you let go, you may not know what to say to your partner, but there is a place to speak. Begin by finding that place, recognize who you are, who you've always been, and who you always will be. If your partner does the same, a portal opens and mutual awakening occurs. Evolutionary relating fulfills our deepest longing — to be completely connected, not only with ourselves and the other person, but with all of existence.

Freedom from Attachment

As we grow and stabilize our essential autonomy, we increasingly become aware of the subtle ways through which we automatically separate ourselves. Remember that when the actual connection is made — soul to soul or essential self to essential self — it is alive and exists whether you are with the other person or not. The connection will become stronger and more ever-present as you and your partner work with these principles.

Soon, you will notice how the ego can create separation by physically taking you away from each other. The ego will say, "I need more space" or it may refuse to make commitments that would allow you and your partner to physically spend more time together. Most often, the ego's strategies have to do with emotional distancing. This is something it does actively, causing you to push your partner away, getting angry, fighting, being disappointed, rejecting your partner, or criticizing and being disrespectful and devaluing the relationship. Or the ego may employ passive techniques, by withdrawing emotionally, stonewalling, not caring, being stubborn and resistant, not communicating, and judging. The ego may even conjure fantasies about leaving your partner, being with someone else, or being alone.

These are all ways in which we close down our hearts and limit what is possible together out of a need to create separation. As we discover and embody essential autonomy, however, the need for automatic distancing will lessen. Our autonomy will provide the strength to be ourselves, share honestly, tolerate differences, and still love our partners fully.

As I've said, this level of relatedness means that you no longer need to push the other away to be yourself. The stabilization in essential autonomy gives the grounding necessary to love fully and be able to detach from ego. As our relationships become more beautiful, the exchanges more intense and enlivening, we will feel how precious, how rare, and how valuable what we have together is. Then, we will weigh losing what we have gained — a sacred attachment to each other and the relationship. Moreover, as the relationship deepens, a rootedness in our essence and the mutual presence with our partner will grow simultaneously.

In addition, your core connection to and love for yourself will help you walk the fine line of not clinging to your partner and knowing that you *could* lose him or her if needed, without losing yourself. If you become overly dependent on your partner, ultimately you won't be able to be your true self. If you are afraid that you might lose the relationship and, as a result, hold on too tightly, not allowing yourself or your partner to be authentic and autonomous, you will end up losing the relationship anyway. Even if you physically stay together, you no longer will relate in an authentic, alive, full way.

Early in my relationship with Peter, over-attachment was something I struggled with. I remember how I felt one weekend when he went to the Hamptons to attend a workshop with our spiritual teacher. I wasn't able to go with him because I needed to be with my son in the city. At this stage of my development, my autonomy was not established deeply enough to balance the intensity of the love I felt for Peter and the profound gift of our growing Evolutionary Relationship. I felt somewhat insecure and jealous, uncomfortable with the idea of Peter going without me, and I told him I wanted him to stay home. He thought about what I said but decided that it felt right for him to go. He left, I stayed at home, and I was furious.

In retrospect, I can see that Peter was more grounded in his essential autonomy, whereas mine was weaker. I therefore was more attached to his presence and felt insecure without him. At that time, I experienced my lack of autonomy as jealously and mistrust. All weekend, I couldn't stop imagining him having fun at the beach, spending time with other women, having new experiences and revelations without me. By the time Peter returned, I was primed to create trouble.

He walked in the door and had barely taken off his jacket when I started questioning him about what happened and who was there. Having spent several days in spiritual practice, he was radiant and centered in himself. When he saw what I was trying to do, he effortlessly deflected my insecure grasping. "Look," he said. "I love you. I love you absolutely and completely. I had an amazing weekend and I would love to be with you and share the space I am in with you. But I can't do that while you are being this way." Then he picked up his jacket and turned toward the door. "I'm going to Central Park. I'll be sitting near the pond where the children sail the toy boats. If you change your mood and you want to be with me, please come. I've missed you." And then he walked out the door ... autonomous and perfectly himself. He wasn't pushing away from me, but neither was he allowing me to pull him into a space of contraction and attachment.

My contracted ego was infuriated. I threw a shoe at the closed door and then sank down against the wall, until I felt my anger and separation slowly melt away. As I regained balance, I was able to feel the growing space of autonomy inside me. I let go of my position of hurt and anger, and soon my need to distance myself from Peter evaporated. Happily, I walked to the park and found the beautiful man I loved. I melted into his arms and we had a glorious afternoon together, merging as one without any grasping or fear, each of us centered in ourselves.

Another way to look at the challenge I confronted with Peter was that I was being asked to let go of attachment. Attachment is an attitude of holding onto a person, an inner posture of grabbing, not wanting to let go. Ironically, attachment is an expression of separateness; it is the desire to cling, to possess that which seems outside ourselves. Evolutionary Relationships can't flourish in an atmosphere where attachment displaces our willingness to risk really showing up and being authentic with our partner. Human beings are unpredictable, so you never know how the other person will react or respond. If we don't remain courageous in being autonomous, we will begin to compromise and collude with each other, and then the relationship will be reduced to two separate egos interacting. To sustain a higher level of relating, it is necessary to stay on the edge of what is real within our self and with our partner. Our mutuality won't survive without our growing autonomy and willingness to confront insecurity.

Of course, as human beings it's natural that we may fear losing each other and, as a result, become attached to those we love. When we are attached, we long for connection, for unity, for the experience of intimacy and closeness. Just listen to any love song and this is what you'll hear: the desire to be one, to never be apart, for nothing to come between us, forever and ever. The original impulse behind attachment is a beautiful one — the desire for unity, which comes from the truth of love. I relish the way this mature love is expressed by Indian revolutionary and mystic Sri Aurobindo:

> Love is a passion and it seeks for two things, eternity and intensity, and in the relation of the Lover and the Beloved. The seeking for eternity and intensity is instinctive and self-born. ... Passing beyond desire for possession, which means a difference, it is seeking for oneness ... two souls merging into each other.[13]

Unfortunately, when the separate ego, which is not rooted in essential autonomy, gets attached, the result is a possessiveness that makes real unity impossible. When we try to possess each other, we turn our partner into a separate object, which means there is no unity. We actually are reinforcing separation, and inevitably this kind of grasping leads to frustration, envy, jealousy, and anger. Until we understand that real union is the absence of boundaries, we unknowingly will create more barriers with our attachments, blocking out the unity that we most deeply want.

Another dimension of autonomy is our capacity to allow the source of love expression through us. Our aim should be to become love and express it uniquely and powerfully into the world. When our hearts are autonomous we love fully without attachment, regardless of whether our love is reciprocated or rejected.

One of my favorite examples of autonomous love comes from the movie *Forrest Gump*, starring Tom Hanks. Forrest, the lead character, has a beautiful, unconditionally open heart when it comes to his beloved Jenny. He unquestionably loves her and it doesn't matter if she leaves him, she is with other men, or she doesn't answer his letters. Forrest just loves her, simply and completely. He resides in his love exactly as it is. He never tries to manipulate circumstances in order to get her or hold her. He also doesn't second-guess his own feelings by shutting down or withdrawing from the pain of loving her. By the end of the movie, Forrest finally joins with Jenny, they have a son together, and their love is mutually shared and expressed.

To have such an autonomous heart is to know your unique connection to love, regardless of how the world and other people respond to your love. It's a place where you are generative, full, and willing to be with your partner without wavering or disconnecting from your essential self. As your Evolutionary Relationship develops and becomes more beautiful and precious, this essential autonomy is the ballast that keeps both of you centered amidst the overwhelming intensity of the intimacy you are swept up into together.

The Dance of Unity and Autonomy

As human beings, we need autonomy and unity, uniqueness and togetherness. The beauty of this paradox is that Evolutionary Relationships bridge these seeming opposites and prove that these mature states can coexist in the space of awakened mutuality.

When we relate from ego, however, autonomy and unity never coexist. They appear as mutually exclusive opposites and in most cases, the best we can do is have one at the expense of the other. Some of us have a preference for independence and separation, and we will sacrifice connection with others in order to maintain it, afraid that if we let other people in, we'll lose our autonomy. Others have a stronger desire for unity and connection and are willing to sacrifice their autonomy, to some degree, in order to maintain their relationships. In such a case, we can become overly accommodating, self-denying, and give ourselves over to the will of the other. We may justify our surrender of autonomy as love, but it actually is driven by a fear of loss.

On an ego level, it's simply not possible to be separate and fully relational at the same time. The best we can do is to create an optimal distance that allows the relationship to stay stable — not too far apart, but not too close. But on an essential level, unity and autonomy exist simultaneously. This is a rare experience, but it's one of the hallmarks of mutual awakening when it occurs between two or more people. Sri Aurobindo, who had a powerful vision of the potential for a collective awakening that he referred to as "the life divine," wrote that in this state, "the cosmic consciousness imbedded in embodied beings would assure a harmonious diversity in oneness."[14]

Spiritual teacher Andrew Cohen, who has done pioneering work with collective awakening, also noted this paradoxical coexistence of qualities as one of the key characteristics of what he called "Evolutionary Enlightenment." Cohen writes:

> The simultaneous emergence of autonomy and communion is a rare and powerful experience. When the barriers between self and other fall away, we experience a higher communion beyond ego boundaries. But when this occurs among people who are awake to the evolutionary impulse, this communion is not just an undifferentiated harmony in which individuality and distinctions are erased. In fact, the very opposite is true. Paradoxically, at the very same time and in the very same space in which we are experiencing profound communion, the autonomy and creative potential of each individual emerges, free from self-consciousness. The simultaneous presence of liberated autonomy and ecstatic communion becomes the defining expression of one experience, one reality.[15]

From a mystical perspective, this paradox is not so surprising, because the mystic understands that the nature of everything is oneness, expressing itself as diversity. The Latin phrase *e pluribus unum* means "out of the many, one" — a sentiment that has been echoed by sages and visionaries for millennia and across all religious traditions. Like waves in the vast ocean of being, each of us is non-separate from ultimate unity, and yet we are each an essential and unique particle of existence, a singular spark of the Divine. When we feel our connection to each other, and at the same time experience our uniqueness, we are accessing the deeper truth of the nature of the cosmos.

In the day-to-day reality of human life, a relationship between two people is always a play between autonomy and unity. Deeply, both coexist in the way I've just described, but on the surface, a relationship that is alive and evolving will include natural fluctuations between autonomy and unity. There will be times when the relationship will be the focus of development and other times when autonomy and individuality are primary. There is a natural ebb and flow that you'll find in each cycle of the relationship, as these seeming opposites dissolve and re-form in new ways. This dance of autonomy and unity will continue over time, sometimes seamlessly merging them, sometimes differentiating, sometimes doing both simultaneously, as you enact, through your connection, the eternal mystery of the one-becoming-many and the many-becoming-one.

One of the promises of evolutionary relating is that it makes it possible to live our divinity here, as a human being on this earth, without waiting until we ascend to some transcendent spiritual realm. Our essential uniqueness is the spark of divine love expressed in each one of us. And our connectedness is the reflection of divine unity that underlies all appearances of separation. A mature human being who has recognized his or her essential uniqueness is able to give fully to life and to other people.

Evolutionary Relationships are not easy, but they are the most rewarding partnerships you can undertake. History contains a long record of special individuals who discovered their uniqueness and were freed to courageously serve life. I believe that we now are being asked to go one step further: to not only find ourselves, but also to find each other and experience and express our collective unity. If "Heaven on Earth" exists, I believe it starts with our capacity for holding both uniqueness and unity.

EXERCISE:
Tincture

This exercise is quite powerful, and it can be shared with one or more people with whom you are experiencing mutual awakening.

Step 1. Begin with a short meditation and allow yourself to fully arrive in this moment. Focus first on yourself, your body, your feelings, and your thoughts. Notice what is arising for you and relax around it. Take your time to locate a sense of intimacy with yourself and know that you are present and available.

Step 2. Now expand your awareness to include your partner(s). With your eyes closed, become aware of how you are sensing your partner(s). Embrace their presence and just allow them to exist in your space and you with them.

Step 3. One person will go first and be the object of focus. This person should simply relax their attention and allow themselves to be seen, known, and exposed. Then, they should invite you and any other partners to connect with the deepest sense of who they are and sense their tincture or "spiritual scent."

Each partner then will share the words that come to them, describing what they sense about the person's tincture. Continue to tune in, to feel the other person. Discover the particular quality of aliveness that emanates from the person, their origination point. Partners may get images, sounds, pictures, lyrics from a song, or other impressions that initially may not make sense. Whatever arises, just say it, and keep focusing on the person and their tincture. Continue sharing observations for about 5 minutes. The person of focus should remain silent and open during this time.

Step 4. Now give the person of focus 5 minutes to share what it was like to feel tuned into and hear the impressions of their tincture. Remember, the content of what your partner(s) shared about you is less important than the experience of having them really pay attention and see you.

Step 5. Switch roles and repeat the exercise so that each participant has the opportunity to be the center of focus. ◌

Notes

1   "A Poet's Advice to Students" in *E. E. Cummings: A Miscellany*, edited by George James Firmage, New York, NY: Argophile Press, 1958, p. 13. First published as a letter Cummings wrote to high school students in *The Ottawa Hills High School Spectator*, October 1955.

2   Agnes De Mille, *Martha: The Life and Work of Martha Graham — A Biography*, New York, NY: Random House, 1991, p. 264.

3   A.H. Almaas, *Essence With the Elixir of Enlightenment: The Diamond Approach to Inner Realization*, Newburyport, MA: Weiser Books, 1998, p. 161.

4   Ibid, p. 162.

5   James Hillman, *The Soul's Code: In Search of Character and Calling*, New York, NY: Grand Central Publishing, 1997, p. 6.

6   Ibid, p. 10.

7   Alan Cohen, *Wisdom of the Heart*, Carlsbad, CA: Hay House, 2002.

8   Cynthia Borgeault, *Love Is Stronger Than Death: The Mystical Union of Two Souls*, Great Barrington, MA: SteinerBooks, 2001, p. 94.

9   Ibid, p. 206.

10 . Martin Buber, *The Way of Man: According to the Teachings of Hasidism*, New York, NY: Citadel Press, 1994, p. 16.

11   Pierre Teilhard de Chardin, *The Future of Man*, New York, NY: Harper & Row, 1964, p. 56.

12   Pierre Teilhard de Chardin, *Human Energy*, New York, NY: Harcourt Brace Jovanovich, 1971, p. 64.

13   Sri Aurobindo, *The Synthesis of Yoga*, Twin Lakes, WI: Lotus Press, 1992, p. 545.

14   Ibid, p. 195.

15   Andrew Cohen, *Evolutionary Enlightenment: A New Path to Spiritual Awakening*, New York, NY: SelectBooks, 2011, p. 192.

CHAPTER TEN
The Seventh Principle: Mutual Influence

Blessed is the influence of one pure, loving human soul on another.

~ George Eliot

One of my favorite memories of Peter is of him sitting on the floor, naked, eating a bowl of tapioca pudding. His body was perfect: six-foot-one, lightly tanned, perfectly proportioned, muscular, strong, but smooth and sensual. In the warmth of a summer afternoon, we sat naked within arm's reach of each other on the floor of our living room in the Hamptons, him leaning against one couch while I leaned against the other at a right angle to him. The sunlight flooded through the open windows, bringing out the red in his wavy brown hair and a sparkle to his intense, penetrating, light blue eyes.

He was looking down at the bowl of tapioca pudding, holding it high and close to his mouth. He lifted the spoon very slowly to his lips, placed it between them, and slowly pulled it out, taking only the smallest amount of pudding onto his tongue. He was totally focused, sensually extracting the full experience of the cool, creamy, sweet pudding. This was how he always ate ... and how he walked ... and how he performed every little task — as though in each moment he was making love to life, with patience, savoring it, and giving himself to it fully.

I started talking to him, playfully laughing and trying to draw him into conversation. He listened but didn't look up. Finally, he patted the rug next to him and said, "Come sit next to me."

I was unaccustomed to anyone telling me what to do like this. "Why?" I asked him.

"Just come over here."

Finally I moved beside him, close enough that our naked bodies were touching.

"How do you feel right now?" he asked.

I started to answer quickly, without thinking, but he stopped me mid-sentence and said quietly, "Close your eyes and really feel where you are."

I could feel something coming to rest within myself. I relaxed, melted into him, and softened. With my eyes closed, I described to him what I was feeling.

"If I hadn't asked you to move closer to me, in a few minutes we would have been in trouble," he said.

I didn't understand what he meant.

"Trust me," he said. "Your conversation, although appearing chatty and playful, was actually subtly challenging and aggressive. You really wanted to be close, to have my attention. You would have created more separation and started taking over."

I felt as if he were seeing through my skin. Not only was my body naked before him, my thoughts and emotions and even some of my unconscious desires were clear to his penetrating gaze. The intimacy of that moment of being seen, deeply, accurately and lovingly, allowed me to melt and want him even more. The half-filled glass dish of pudding was placed carefully on the coffee table. He reached out to me. I was now the entire focus of his attention: his body, his mouth, and his incredible consciousness. The essence of his soul was fully present and awakened in the very cells of his body. And thus, he awakened mine.

Peter influenced me, and I him, in ways I had never imagined possible. Throughout the all-too-short time we had together, Peter and I continuously grew in our individual and dual capacity to be awake, sensitive, and open to the influence we shared at each moment.

The memories of that afternoon (and many others) are crystal clear to me even decades later, because in those simple times together, I learned so much about the power of relating. Peter's presence and sensitivity to such moments and his commitment to guiding and influencing me left a deep impression. He had an unusually developed capacity to be truly intimate with his own experience and a commitment to share that depth with me. Had it been otherwise, Peter would have eaten his pudding unconsciously, I would have demanded his attention, and eventually we'd have gotten into an argument and related to each other as separate selves in a normal but very limited and shallow state of consciousness. Twenty years later, there would have been nothing to remember, no influence that deepened our relationship or affected how we evolved together.

What I learned from my relationship with Peter is that we can touch each other and affect each other deeply and irrevocably. I have come to call this "mutual influence" — the Seventh Activating Principle of Evolutionary Relationships.

Evolutionary Relationships are dependent on our willingness and conscious embrace of the power of influence. As we develop our awareness of influence — the ways we influence each other and our capacity to be influenced — we begin to realize that we are experiencing a new field of consciousness. This field eventually becomes a way of being, a sensitivity akin to that of an orchestra conductor, who can simultaneously hear, appreciate, and coordinate many levels of melody, harmony, rhythm, sound, and vibration. Consequently, mutual influence is the most precious dimension of any relationship.

Take a moment to reflect on those who have had a profound influence on you and your life. How has their love, brilliance, commitment, and support shaped you at the deepest levels? What aspects of yourself have been molded by their touch, by their very existence? Imagine what your life would have been like without their influence. When I consider those people who have influenced me most profoundly — my mother, Peter, my teacher Werner Erhard — I can't imagine who I might be without having known them. My sense of self was changed forever by the imprint of those relationships.

A common definition of influence is "the capacity or power of persons or things to be a compelling force on or produce effects on the actions, behavior, and opinions of others." To me, however, "force" is not the best descriptor of how influence occurs. In physics, a force is any influence that causes an object to undergo a certain change concerning its movement, direction, or geometrical construction. In human relationships, influence is not the forceful imposition of one person's will, opinions, or beliefs on another; it is a more subtle dance between two souls. Let's look at the root of the word, which comes from the Latin word *influere*, meaning "to flow into." Influence is the way in which we flow into each other, like streams whose waters meet, mingle, and then converge, each assuming some part of the other.

In our culture, where individuality and originality are so highly valued, we're trained to resist influence and "think for ourselves." When we are young and striving to craft our identities, such encouragement makes sense and is healthy. We all cherish the freedom to create our own destiny, and rightly so. Oftentimes, our unique expression is hard won, since many of us have been let down or betrayed by people we trusted but who influenced us in negative ways. We've learned the hard way not to be too vulnerable to others, to resist the kind of influence that manipulates, forces, projects, or originates from the ego of another.

On the other hand, while there's great value in cultivating our independence, we can take it too far. We can fail to acknowledge and embrace the truth that we actually live in a web of influence, where we are continuously influenced by and influencing others. Instead, we can be open to expanding our sense of personal freedom and self-determination to include our love and profound connectedness to each other. Additionally, we can become more thoughtful, sensitive, intentional, and considerate in the ways we influence others. For those of us who have sufficiently developed our individuality, self-esteem, and independence, this is the new frontier.

Opening to Influence

How can we become more aware of and open to influence? First, we need to acknowledge that we influence each other on multiple levels — from the most obvious to the very subtle — with most of the influence invisible to our current (more linear, superficial) awareness. Our impact on others is not limited to the ways in which we consciously try to influence them. Unconscious or semi-conscious attitudes, emotions, and beliefs influence others without either person being aware of what is occurring. Even our physical states influence each other. Embracing our power of influence, learning how it functions and how we can engage its power consciously, with love, sensitivity and focus, is critical in developing this next level of consciousness.

> *The reason we are able to influence each other so deeply is that our souls are innately permeable to one another. While each of us are distinct individuals, we also interface with each other in a field of unlimited possibilities.*

The contemporary spiritual teacher A.H. Almaas writes, "As far as I can tell, we are the only beings who are permeable to everything that exists, from the most painful to the most sublime."[1] Almaas adds that "our uniquely human quality of vulnerability is a disadvantage from one perspective and a great advantage from another. We're wide open to all influences, all possibilities if we allow ourselves to be — if we don't defend ourselves, if we don't build a shell and hide behind it."

In an Evolutionary Relationship, we strive to embrace our vulnerability from the perspective of it being a profound advantage which allows us to open ourselves fully to influence within a consciously created environment of trust, transparency, and the mutual desire to evolve. When we are open to it, we can experience mutuality as a physical sensation, a tingling aliveness to the interplay of influence between us.

The Many Ways We Touch

The quality of our relationships profoundly impacts each one of us. Human beings are social creatures. From the moment we enter this world, we are connected to others, and almost every aspect of our development is informed by our interactions with those around us, even the physical development of our brain, as neuroscientists have recently shown. It is a powerful practice to simply pay attention to all the ways in which you are being influenced on a daily basis, by other people and by your environment.

For example, the weather may influence your emotional states, or the seasons of the year may affect you differently. It also has been shown that the phases of the moon exert powerful, unseen influence on our bodies and minds. In *The Bond*, Lynne McTaggart summarizes fascinating research on lunar influences, including evidence that violent crimes increase during a full or new moon, psychiatric patients have fewer psychotic episodes during a full moon, and workers tend to be absent from their jobs during a full moon.[2]

I have a dear friend who is an emergency medicine physician at New York Hospital, and he agrees with McTaggart's research. He is in charge of scheduling the hospital staff's work shifts, and he has noticed that many of the employees don't want to work during the full moon. Notice how your environment influences you, including the food you eat and the culture in which you surround yourself. As you awaken to these outside factors, you will bring into focus the inescapable network of mutuality that connects you with nature, with the cosmos, and with the people and culture around you.

For most people, relationships are the most powerful conduits of influence. We influence each other all the time, whether we are conscious of it or not. In his book *Outliers*, Malcolm Gladwell tells the story of a small Italian town called Roseto, where families stay closely connected, cooking together and caring for each other. A doctor noticed that in this town, no one under fifty-five years of age has ever died of a heart attack, and the rates of heart disease are dramatically lower than elsewhere in Italy. In addition, there are no cases of suicide or addiction, and the town has an exceedingly low crime rate. Yet, the most interesting fact about this town is that residents aren't living a so-called "healthy" lifestyle. They eat high-fat foods and even smoke. What this town demonstrates, Gladwell writes, is "the idea that community — the values of the world we inhabit and the people we surround ourselves with — has a profound effect on who we are."[3] Many studies have chronicled the same phenomenon, including several which show that people are much more likely to become obese if their friends are obese.

The first step in engaging with the power of influence is simply to become aware of the kinds of influence that already are occurring. In small ways, we are influenced by each other on a daily basis. Have you ever experienced a time when someone looked at you with love and appreciation, and in that moment you felt changed? Or perhaps you're struggling with a project or a difficult life transition. In such a case, simply having another person in your life providing encouragement and inspiration can make all the difference in your ability to persevere. Conversely, if someone you are close to is sad or depressed, you may find yourself mirroring their emotional state, even though you personally have nothing to be sad about. In the same way, a close friend's happiness or contentment may unexpectedly uplift or soothe you.

The influence we have on each other's emotional states is not limited to direct contact with single individuals, but extends throughout our extended social network. According to a thirty-year longitudinal study from Harvard University, which followed more than 12,000 people who were all part of one interconnected network, our chances of being happy increase by 15% if a direct connection in our network is happy. Even more interesting, the study found that *indirect* connections influence happiness as well. For instance, if a friend of our direct connection is happy, our odds of being happy increase by 10% even if we don't know or interact with that person. Influence was even shown to extend to friends of friends of friends! One of the researchers, Nicholas Christakis, summed up their findings: "People are embedded in social networks and the health and wellbeing of one person affects the health and wellbeing of others. ... Human happiness is not merely the province of isolated individuals."[4]

Every relationship has a field that is distinct and bigger than either individual. This relational field may be stagnant, in which case it is experienced as dull or heavy. Or the relationship may be stable, and while we may appreciate the stability, as we become more awake, we will sense the fixed patterns and may perceive the field as deadlocked. Such non-evolving relationships inevitably are destructive, since they keep both people stuck and limit our sense of possibility and aliveness. Conversely, when the relational field is dynamic and thriving, we feel the relationship as transformative and empowering. When we have relationships like this, we have only to come close to the person to feel more awake, uplifted, and in touch with a greater sense of possibility.

Influence of this magnitude impacts us on more than just emotional and psychological levels. Research from the relatively new field of interpersonal neurobiology shows that our brains constantly rewire themselves and that one of the most powerful factors prompting change is our relationships. This impact begins at birth, with the influence of our parents or caregivers, and it continues throughout our lives. The brain remains flexible, as the imprint of our close relationships and our interactions with others shape our neural pathways, including those that are genetically programmed. According to Daniel J. Siegel, originator of interpersonal neurobiology, brain-altering communication is triggered by deeply felt emotions that register in facial expressions, eye contact, touch, posture, movements, pace and timing, intensity, and tone of voice.[5]

Besides our brains, other aspects of our physicality are highly susceptible to the influence of other people. Studies have shown that when couples in a healthy relationship hold their partner's hand, their blood pressure is lessened, stress is reduced, overall health improves, and physical pain softens. A 2005 study of forty-two couples demonstrated that when a small wound was inflicted on one partner, those who reported having stress and hostility in their relationship took almost twice as long to heal compared to those who reported being in a loving and happy relationship. Siegel notes that "Scientific studies of longevity, medical and mental health, happiness and even wisdom point to supportive relationships as the most robust predictor of these positive attributes in our lives across the life span."[6]

A Love You Never Get Over

Most of us have experienced losing someone whom we've loved deeply. Nevertheless, we experience their influence throughout the remainder of our lives. Our capacity to influence each other is not limited to a shared lifetime. It's a gift we leave long after we are gone, since our love for each other is lasting and real. As Winston Churchill once said, "The influence of each human being on others in this life is a kind of immortality."

Within the last decade, I have lost my parents, a favorite aunt, and my two beloved cats of fourteen and seventeen years who both died in my arms. In the face of the stark and strangely beautiful reality of death, the elegance and exuberance of life becomes especially vivid and undeniable. With each loss, I comprehend more deeply that the most precious element of human life is the fact that we can love each other in ways that change us forever. Often when we lose a loved one, either to death or a breakup, we try to "get over" that person in order to "move on" with our lives. This rudimentary impulse denies not only the most powerful aspect of our relatedness, but the deeper truth that our relatedness continues.

It's possible to be "un-get-over-able" in terms of the influence we have on each other. Evolutionary Relationships are an expression of love we never get over, and never want to. It's natural to continue to feel the influence and support of such a significant relationship, even if we no longer are together. Such lasting influence doesn't have to prevent us from being open to new love and new relationships. Pushing away the lingering positive influence of a lost partner in order to "move on" takes an enormous amount of psychic energy that usually hurts us in the long run and never works anyway.

It's been more than twenty-five years since I first watched Peter move slowly toward me on the dance floor, his intense blue eyes holding mine. When we were together, I experienced our love as a presence that infused my very cells, influencing me constantly. In fact, I felt him all the time, even when we were separated by thousands of miles. One time, he was in Germany and I was in New York. I missed him and started to cry. Immediately the phone rang, and before I could say anything he asked, "What's wrong?"

Synchronous events like this happened often and, after a while, ceased to surprise me. Peter helped me understand and live the reality that we are part of an invisible, interconnected field of intelligence. Even when Peter and I first met, our connection was instantaneous. "Lovers don't finally meet somewhere. They're in each other all along," wrote Rumi.[7] That's how it felt. Even now, Peter is here, influencing my heart and my work. I still find it amazing that the unique chemistry of our coming together has evoked a sustained intensity of love that continues to this day.

Interestingly, there is a parallel phenomenon that scientists have observed in the realm of quantum physics, known as "entanglement." Some researchers have described it as the quantum equivalent of telepathy. First proposed in the 1930s by Niels Bohr, the Theory of Entanglement states that once subatomic particles have been connected or paired, they can be separated by time and distance yet continue to affect each other. No force or energy needs to be present. Einstein was uncomfortable with entanglement, which he described as the particles' "spooky action at a distance."

Today, Bohr's theory has been proven. In 1997, Dr. Nicolas Gisin and his colleagues at the University of Geneva conducted a twin-photon experiment in which pairs of photons were shot in opposite directions to villages north and south of Geneva along optical fibers like those used to transmit telephone calls. When the photons reached the ends of these fibers, they were forced to make random choices between alternative and equally possible pathways. The paired photons always made the same decisions, even though no explanation could be found in the laws of classical physics that would account for such "nonlocal" coordination/communication.

Many people view quantum entanglement as scientific proof of the underlying interconnectedness of all life. While I am not a scientist and hesitate to draw overly simplistic parallels between quantum physics and spiritual concepts, I do find this example to be, at the very least, a powerful metaphor for the kind of "entanglement" we experience in our relationships. And it has helped me understand why certain deep relationships are never "over," even when we sometimes would like them to be.

Finally, entanglement is not just a romantic notion; it is a sobering one. If we really are together forever, even beyond death, do we need to consciously nurture and care for our relationships after our loved one has passed or our partner leaves? Having recently ended a four-year relationship with a man I was engaged to marry, I'm deeply grateful for our capacity to remain true to the love and connection we still have, even though our life journey looks very different now than we had once hoped. I love him and continue to feel the influence of his love for me, our mutual acceptance, and our deep support of each other's journey.

Becoming a Connoisseur of Influence

As you develop in an Evolutionary Relationship, you will become a connoisseur of influence. Think about someone who has a highly developed palate for wine, like a sommelier in a high-end restaurant. She can describe subtleties of flavor and aroma that you may not be able to distinguish, and she knows how a whole sequence of factors have influenced the particular character of the wine in your glass: the climate, the geographical area where the grapes were grown, the moment when the winemaker chose to pick them, the type of soil, the kind of oak barrels, and how long the wine has aged.

Similarly, it's possible to develop a "palate" for relatedness, where you become highly attuned to the qualities of the field between you and another person, where you are aware of all the factors that have influenced and continue to influence that field. Every intention, conscious and unconscious, affects the field. Literally everything we share or hold back leaves an imprint. Our individual states of mind, our integrity, our willingness to be open, our degree of commitment, our vulnerability, our intensity of engagement — all of these factors are interconnected and influence the field.

Consequently, it is easy to ruin this field and the relationship that exists within it by not being sensitive to how our conscious and unconscious intentions are influencing the space between us. Just as bad weather or too much oak can ruin a good wine, our relationship can be jeopardized when we are careless or reckless. As a result, we need to become acutely aware of the power of influence and sensitive to all of the factors that play a part in creating the field.

Learning how to influence each other with clarity of consciousness and the ability to reflect back to each other the influence that is occurring is a subtle dance that must be mastered in order for our Evolutionary Relationship to evolve.

Ironically, one of the elements that can ruin a newly developing relationship is pushing too hard to create a fertile field. For instance, you and your partner need to be aware of each other's capacity for passion or depth. If too much is shared or exchanged without the shared field being able to hold what is happening, the relationship could collapse. People often don't understand why a partnership that showed so much promise fell apart, but this often is why.

With patience, we become capable of growing and refining the field of relatedness. This sophistication of perception is a dimension of consciousness that needs to be developed and practiced. It includes elements of clarity, sensuousness, and access to many layers of comprehension to discern the real from the unreal. It is a mystical awakening, activated together, that is alive and practical. Once properly stimulated, the field of our relatedness will unfold organically. In an Evolutionary Relationship, awareness of influence requires a constant feedback loop, where we circulate our recognition of what is occurring between us and our response to it, so that the field becomes more conscious, vivid, and intentional.

The Shape of Relationships

What is the "shape" of your relationship? That may seem like a strange question, but it points to an important distinction when studying the power of influence. Relationships come in different sizes and shapes. To start, there are symmetrical relationships and there are asymmetrical relationships. In a symmetrical relationship, you experience a certain degree of balance. Each partner operates on a similar developmental level and is capable of exerting an equal degree of influence with the other. You might have such a relationship with your spouse or lover, or with a close sibling, business partner, or friend.

In an asymmetrical relationship, however, there is a fundamental imbalance between the partners. One person may have a far greater degree of influence over the other or be more conscious and attuned to what is happening in the relationship. Examples of these types of relationships include teacher and student, parent and child, or therapist and patient.

Of course, every relationship is different, and there always will exist areas of balance and areas of imbalance. But it is important to make this distinction if you are interested in creating an Evolutionary Relationship, because the degree of symmetry in any particular connection affects the dynamic of the relationship and what is possible.

Imagine that you are a tennis player and you want to play a satisfying and challenging match. You will look for an opponent who is close to your own skill level — perhaps a little better but not too much — so that you can experience the excitement of connecting through the interaction of skill and athleticism. However, if you play a match against someone whose skill level is far below yours, your experience of the game will be different. You may enjoy coaching your opponent, but you will not experience the same challenge you would with a peer. Similarly, if you play a tennis expert, you will be developmentally challenged, but you will not experience that same thrill as you would when equally matched. It might even be frustrating and disappointing to play a tennis expert, especially if you had hoped that there was symmetry in your capacity to play the match.

Relationships work the same way. The more symmetrical the relationship, the more partners will be attuned to each other and able to connect their capacities. The same is true in the art of lovemaking. When there is balance in the two partners' sexual experience, as well as trust and openness, they can confidently regulate each other's experience: create excitement, move the energy in different directions, experiment and respond. They can share a mutual experience in a field of pleasure, love, and dynamic relatedness. If one partner is more sexually, spiritually, or energetically developed, however, then they naturally will take a more active role, regulate the situation, and guide the other, less practiced lover. It still might be a pleasurable connection for both partners, but the experience will not feel mutually balanced.

When it comes to Evolutionary Relationships, the important set of skills for symmetry and balance includes: commitment, engagement, truth, transparency, intimacy, sensitivity, influence, openness, trust, and true autonomy. For example, if I am in a relationship with a man, I would ask myself: *Do we have an equal capacity to be sensitive to each other and to the field of our relationship?* If we do, then I should be aware of his energy, his mood shifts, and when he's more distant. Similarly, he should be able to sense when I'm anxious or flighty. Simply put, we should be able to track each other and experience mutuality and symmetry. And because we are attuned to each other, we can intentionally influence each other in subtle but powerful ways. If I sense him feeling sad and pulling away, I can give him my energy and attention in ways that support him and bring him close again. If he feels me getting flighty, he might take a couple deep breaths and calm the space between us, and *voila*, all of a sudden I feel grounded again.

By way of contrast, in an asymmetrical relationship, like that between a mother and child, the mother is fully and acutely attuned to her child, constantly tracking his needs, his physical and emotional states, his energy levels, and so on. The child is unaware of this, however, and does not reciprocate his mother's level of attunement. Or imagine a relationship between a therapist and a patient. When the patient sits on the therapist's couch, he is not worried about how the therapist is feeling, but the therapist is completely attuned to the patient.

Some friendships are asymmetrical too. Do you have certain friends whom you feel attuned to and concerned about, but who never seem to reciprocate that degree of awareness and interest in you? If you've had a relationship with a narcissist, you certainly have experienced being on the short end of the stick, because narcissists are not attuned to anyone but themselves and seek the attention of others. Asymmetrical relationships aren't necessarily bad or lacking in value, but they have certain limitations. It is important to be able to recognize their limitations, so that you don't have unrealistic expectations about what's possible in these relationships.

If you want to create an Evolutionary Relationship, you and your partner will need to cultivate *mutual influence*, which means the conscious desire, willingness, and capacity to be influenced by one another. In order to do this, you must become aware of the shape of your particular relationship so that you can use the power of influence creatively and effectively. Think about one of your relationships that is meaningful for you. Pay attention to the places where you meet. It might be during physical activities that you both experience a similar level of engagement and accomplishment — like golfing together or skiing. When you are golfing or skiing, you are able to share this dimension of life with a sense of challenge and excitement. It may even open up new ways of knowing and loving each other.

Or your meeting place could be in the realm of emotional depth and spiritual sensitivity. Perhaps both of you share a deep commitment to meditation or yoga, supporting each other in silence and mystical discovery. There are countless places you may meet: in humor, intellectual curiosity, creativity, capacities for sexual depth, intimacy, or love.

As you identify these meeting points, try to sense into what the resulting field feels like. *Are you maximizing the potential of those places where symmetry unfolds? Could you "push the edge" together by bringing more attention to those places?* When you have symmetry, there is a much greater potential for new discoveries to be made and uncharted territory to be explored together. And when you meet on the edge of that space, the evolutionary force starts to move through and between you. That's what makes an Evolutionary Relationship so extraordinary.

During this process, you may become aware of places in your relationship where there is not symmetry. That's okay. It's not a problem. In fact, it may represent fertile ground for more personal growth and an opportunity for deepening the relationship. Remember, the richness of the relationship is generated by giving and receiving.

Let's say, for example, you are in a beautiful friendship, where you deeply meet in many dimensions and feel ready to embark on a journey of mutual influence and evolution. But you recognize that your friend seems to have more access to integrity than you do. Perhaps in your particular life journey, you have not fully developed or possibly even valued integrity and impeccability, while your partner's journey supported that development. If you acknowledge that there is asymmetry in this dimension of the relationship, you can utilize the relationship as the vehicle for your development in the domain of integrity. You can be open to an exchange, and you can learn from your partner in a very beautiful way.

By recognizing our strengths and weaknesses and not pretending to be equal with our partner in every way, we encourage a beautiful dance of influence between us that enlivens and enriches us both. However, if we don't recognize the opportunity that asymmetry provides, we easily can fall into patterns of competition or become judgmental, frustrated, and defensive.

When we openly acknowledge
our strengths and weaknesses, we honor
the influence of our partner.
By being humble, we find that each of us has
different domains of development to share.

In this way, asymmetry is an important dimension of an Evolutionary Relationship, though it needs to be balanced by areas in which both partners feel fully met as peers. Otherwise the relationship may become one-sided, and its deeper potentials won't be able to unfold. Therefore, it is best to come together with a significant degree of symmetry. Then, your capacities will unfold together, and the optimizing force will be activated to take both of you somewhere new.

Once the optimizing force awakens in and through your relationship, you will be inside of something greater than both of you that actually is discovering itself through you. This happens, for example, when two brilliant scientists open and join genius. They then find themselves sharing a field wherein discoveries and insights never could have been accessed alone. Similarly, two masterful dancers may find themselves in the field and carried by the flow of the music, as if they are "being danced" rather than dancing. Or lovers, like Peter and me, may simultaneously access their own and each other's feelings and sensations and move into a sea of unified consciousness that envelopes and carries them into mystical dimensions.

Remember, each relationship is unique and has its own potentials and limitations. You can't decide ahead of time what they are. You first have to discover what is there — which elements are asymmetrical and which are symmetrical — and then let the truth and the optimizing force dictate what actually is possible.

Our capacity for influence is a great gift and a great responsibility. As the wonderful spiritual pioneer Irina Tweedie writes in *Daughter of Fire*:

The realization that every act, every word, every thought of ours not only influences our environment but for some mysterious reason forms an integral and important part of the Universe, fits into it as if by necessity so to say, in the very moment we do, or say, or think it — is an overwhelming and even shattering experience.

The tremendous responsibility of it is terrifying.

If all of us only knew that the smallest act of ours, or a tiny thought, has such far-reaching effects as to set in motion forces which perhaps could shatter a galaxy. ...

If we know it deeply and absolutely, if this realization becomes engraved permanently on our hearts, on our minds, how careful we would act and speak and think. How precious life would become in its integral oneness.[8]

Are you ready to open yourself to this potential and responsibility? Are you willing to be consciously open, to allow another person's words, emotions, and actions to influence you? Are you willing to be affected, to care, to be vulnerable and transparent? Are you prepared to extend yourself, to be generous, to take a risk and maybe change another person's life forever?

All of us have devoted significant time to developing independence and individuality, to fulfilling our personal needs and desires. Now it's time for us to discover our interdependence. It's time to open ourselves to the beauty of how we can love each other, create together, and be unforgettable in each other's lives.

Notes

1   A.H. Almaas, *Diamond Heart Book III: Being and the Meaning of Life*, Boulder, CO: Shambhala Publications, 2000, p. 197.

2   Lynne McTaggart, *The Bond: How to Fix Your Falling-Down World*, New York, NY: Atria Books, 2012.

3   Malcolm Gladwell, *Outliers: The Story of Success*, New York, NY: Back Bay Books, 2011, p. 12.

4   J.H. Fowler and N.A. Christakis, "Dynamic Spread of Happiness in a Large Social Network: Longitudinal Analysis over 20 Years in the Framingham Heart Study," 2008, *BMJ*, 337: a2338. Online at http://www.bmj.com/content/337/bmj.a2338.

5   Diane Ackerman, "The Brain on Love," *The New York Times*, March 24, 2012. Online edition at https://opinionator.blogs.nytimes.com/2012/03/24/the-brain-on-love.

6   Ibid.

7   *The Essential Rumi*, translated by Coleman Barks, London, UK: Penguin, 1999, p. 106.

8   Irina Tweedie, *Daughter of Fire: A Diary of a Spiritual Training with a Sufi Master*, Point Reyes Station, CA: The Golden Sufi Center, 1995, p. 812.

CHAPTER ELEVEN
The Eighth Principle: Contact

I remember that time you told me you said, "Love is touching souls."
Surely you touched mine 'cause part of you
pours out of me in these lines from time to time.
Oh, you're in my blood like holy wine; You taste so bitter and so sweet.
Oh I could drink a case of you darling; And I would still be on my feet.

~ Joni Mitchell, *Case of You*

I met the amazing futurist Barbara Marx Hubbard in 1999 and, like thousands of people who have been in her presence, felt inspired by her embodied vision of conscious evolution, her contagious liveliness, and formidable brilliance. Buckminster Fuller said of her, "There is no doubt in my mind that Barbara Marx Hubbard — who helped introduce the concept of futurism to society — is the best informed human now alive regarding futurism and the foresights it has produced."

On the first day Barbara and I met, even before she spoke, I felt an innate alignment with her on a soul level that mystified me. As we got to know each other and I learned more about her vision and perspective on conscious evolution, I moved to Santa Barbara and we worked together for close to a year. It has been a destinal relationship, with its meaning still unfolding. We've stayed in touch over the years, given some talks together, and have been supportive of each other's work.

When I moved to the Bay Area, Barbara told her sister Patricia Ellsberg, who lives in Berkeley, to contact me. Patricia and I met over dinner, and I felt a deep connection with her as well. This was interesting to me, because I've never had a sister, yet I felt a kind of sisterhood with Patricia immediately.

Recently, Barbara came to visit me and the connection between us went somewhere very new. We did the Mutual Awakening Practice together, and as we looked into each other's eyes and touched each other's souls, a depth of exchange surged between us, leaving us both not only euphoric, but deeply impacted by the reality of our innate connection.

Like Barbara, I have surrendered fully to the guidance of something greater. Consequently, with her I feel a strong sense of unity that comes from the same source, a similar mission, and the recognition and exchange that we share. One can only speculate where it might lead us now, since our contact catalyzed latent potentials that awaited our coming together. I am grateful for the gift of being connected to such an exquisite woman, and I treasure that our mutual recognition is so complete.

When we are touched at the soul level by another human being, we never forget it. It might not be a physical touch and nothing explicit may be said or done, but when someone comes into contact with our soul, it makes an indelible impression. Sometimes the smallest encounter stays with us for decades because, however brief, it was a moment of real contact.

Often, human connection is taken for granted, but as we've discussed in earlier chapters, it's actually quite rare for two individuals to meet each other at an essential level — origination point to origination point. Contact, the way I use the term, means touching each other with our core being, with the substance of our consciousness. It's a profound form of intimacy that requires both parties to be fully present in order to step outside the conventional experience of human relationships. Contact includes the experience of shared touch — where partners simultaneously feel each other and the contact itself. Contact includes the conscious ability to transmit the fullness of our essence through a look or physical touch, or through our voice or even silence. Contact feels intensely personal, tender, unfiltered, raw, and unmistakable. You know with certainty that you have touched and been touched by the other person — poignant and simple. Unfortunately, most of the time we don't make real contact with each other. Our self-images interact but not our souls.

Some people are more capable than others at reaching this deeper level of relating, but the essential prerequisite for contact to occur is that each individual must be present in their own unique essence or origination point, as described in Chapter Nine. When we identify with the ego, we relate to others as objects through the filter of the ego's constructed images. Contact occurs beyond ego, but it is not the same as merging into unity consciousness, which may occur, for example, during a shared spiritual experience. When we contact another person beyond ego, we may lose awareness of our separation and experience shared consciousness, but there still are two distinct individuals who are allowing themselves to be seen and touched. Ego boundaries are eliminated, but individuation is maintained. The result is a shared and simultaneous experience of oneness, distinctness and contact, where one person's essence is touching another's. We feel it not simply as a subjective connection, but in a way that is as real and as tangible as physical contact.

Essential contact can arise during many forms of interaction — sitting in silence, talking on the phone, working creatively together, making love, or exploring ideas in deep conversation — whenever we actually touch soul-to-soul. One real moment of contact can leave you forever altered. And if you are fortunate, it can develop into a more constant state of connection where you feel the closeness and contact even when your partner is not physically with you.

Most interactions are either unconscious or partly conscious. When we move across the surface of life, focused on being efficient and getting things done, we pay little attention to our interactions. There's nothing wrong with that per se, though it's a more utilitarian way to relate to each other. However, it is important to know the difference and to be aware of what is happening in the moment. Another definition of contact is being awake, sensitized, intentional, and able to transmit the fullness of your essence through a look, touch, or speech. Contact occurs when the other person feels with certainty that you are touching who they are at the core. It is an intentional tenderness and it stops people in their tracks. It also disrupts superficial realities and plunges individuals into a deeper, shared reality with each other. Something real has been shared and you both know it.

True contact is a soul level experience that is profoundly and unmistakably felt by both people in the relationship. Once established, the connection is permanent — a poignant reminder of those whom we have loved at a soul level.

I have experienced soulful contact in many of my relationships. During my teen years, I experienced it with my first boyfriend, whose essence stayed with me long after we broke up. In fact, I continue to feel an ongoing connection with him. Even after years of not seeing him, when he unexpectedly appeared at my doorstep one day, the vividness of our connection immediately returned. With Peter I felt it the most powerfully, and I continue to feel close contact with him to this day, more than twenty years after his death — truly magical.

I also experience deep contact with close friends, especially a woman with whom I have an Evolutionary Relationship. When she and I go for a walk together or have a glass of wine in a favorite restaurant, I feel a heightened sensory awareness of temperature, texture, taste, light, form, and aesthetics — and she feels it too. We are inside the experience together, paying attention to the space between us and the shared sense of being alive and awake. With this friend, we mutually share the experience of beauty; it's something that is particular to and enhanced by our connection. With another friend, whom I've known and loved for twenty-five years, we slip inside a different place where humor shapes our shared experience. As a result, our contact often incorporates the repartee of laughter and seeing the comedy of life all around us.

Some of us have experienced exceptional contact with an animal. My cat Austin was incredibly present and loved to connect with me. He would stare at me as I moved about the apartment, and if I walked over to where he was lying and curled up beside him, he would hold my gaze and then reach his paw out, very deliberately, and touch my cheek. If I leaned into him, he would continue looking at me, tilting his head slightly, and then close his eyes, while leaving his paw on my face. We really felt each other and relished the poignancy of our contact through such simple exchanges. Think about times when you've really made contact — with an animal friend or a human. It's vivid and unmistakable. You remember where you were, what happened, and the intense feeling of love and connection. The very contours of the experience are impressed on your soul.

Occasionally, I experience contact with a total stranger — like an elderly woman I saw on the street, slowly maneuvering her walker through the bustling sidewalk of New York's midtown at lunchtime. It was as though the sea of pedestrians parted around us. As our eyes locked I saw her — *really saw her* — and I knew she saw me too. In those few moments when our eyes locked, the essence of who she was touched me, and I felt a wave of tremendous respect for her quiet strength and dignity. We stood there and paused ... and then we moved on. The experience brought me to tears. I don't know who she was or where she was going, but her impression is still with me now as I share the experience with you. And I relive the contact in an instant, whenever I recall the encounter.

For most of us, experiences like this are rare and usually only occur with people we are very close to — most often with a lover. In the current paradigm of relating, human beings almost never experience being deeply seen or deeply touched, but in the field of evolutionary relating, we discover that what once felt rare and extraordinary becomes more natural.

However, it's important to be aware that given our inexperience in this domain, we easily can feel overwhelmed or confused by this deep level of contact. It's also possible to misinterpret its meaning. Often, when people initially experience powerful contact, they think, "I must be falling in love! What does this mean?" Yet, as they become more accustomed to the experience, they eventually realize that it does not necessarily imply a romantic or sexual connection. Rather, they begin to discern the natural form of that relationship, and they do this by staying open and paying attention to the particular qualities of that connection.

One of my most unexpected experiences of contact occurred with a massage therapist whom I went to see in Santa Fe, about five years after Peter died. This masseur was a masterful healer, and as he worked on me, I sensed that he was adept at being fully present through his hands. It was a normal massage, except that I experienced him making real contact with me on the inner planes. As I lay there, my body was able to receive the contact of essential presence in a way I hadn't experienced since Peter's death. My depth was touched and I felt nourished and grateful to feel myself touched in that way again.

When the massage ended, I thanked him and told him how much I appreciated his capacity for "contact." Then I asked him what he experienced, and he said, "I'll love you forever." What was exquisite about this exchange is that we both had enough maturity in the domain of sensitivity and presence to receive what happened with discernment (i.e., without romantic fantasies or sexual innuendo). The next day I was catapulted into a meditative ecstatic state that lasted six hours. A year later, when I moved to Santa Fe and we became friends, he told me that he had powerful dreams and an altered consciousness for two days after our initial encounter. I realized that in the short time we spent together, existence had made it possible for two people capable of advanced contact to catalyze spiritual awakenings needed by both. Today, I wonder what might have transpired between us if, as friends, we had shared the Mutual Awakening Practice.

Learning to accept new forms of intimacy and connection is a wonderful challenge. It also is a gift as we move into higher levels of development as human beings. The intensity and richness of contact fills a deep void within us — a place where we hunger for connection but may have become acclimated to not receiving what we need.

Levels of Contact

Contact occurs on several different levels: energetic, physical, emotional, and mental. However, it is the individual's connection with essence or origination point that brings alive these various forms of contact, filling them with presence and power. If we are not fully present as our essential self, then our points of contact with others will be lacking and devoid of substance. Ultimately, the degree of contact is dependent not on what we do with the other person, but on how much essential presence we bring to the interaction and exchange. When both partners are fully present, they will experience profound contact, even if thousands of miles apart. Let's take a closer look at these different levels of connection, and explore what it feels like when the connection is infused with essential presence.

Physical Contact

There are many ways to make contact through our physical senses. One of the most powerful ways is through the eyes. It has been said, "The eyes are the window to the soul." No doubt, this phrase has resonated for eons because of its primordial truth. When we look into the eyes of our partner, we do see more deeply what is "inside."

Lovers naturally feel comfortable with the intimacy of looking into each other's eyes. So much transpires through a gaze, through "eye contact." A world of communication can be exchanged without a word being spoken. When we are angry with someone or we wish to deceive, we often don't want to make eye contact.

In spiritual circles, the practice of "eye-gazing" has become something of a cliché, but it isn't merely a feel-good, sentimental way to connect. Looking deeply into the eyes of another person is one of the most powerful ways to see who is there and make contact. It's also one of the easiest ways to initiate contact, soul to soul. We are designed to find each other and know each other through sight. In the movie *Avatar*, the blue indigenous beings say to each other, "I see you," when they proclaim their connection. My experience is that once I truly "see" another person, both us are taken to a new world of intimacy and awakening.

You may be surprised by the power of this simple practice. A friend and I once had a profound experience during a gazing session we shared. Here's how he described our contact:

> *I was enraptured in a world of liquid light, golden ribbons of stardust that seemed to be falling from invisible heavens. It was bathing us in luminosity, or rather, we were beings of pure luminous form. I was held in rapture for a few precious minutes seeing a world formed of liquid light. I had no thoughts about it at the time, but afterward I realized that I had been gifted with a poetic and metaphoric image of the world as it already exists in unmanifest possibility and will exist in future manifestation. It was a world of wonder and awe, a perfectly communicated union of individuality flowing in an intricate dance of coherence and chaos.*

Of course, it's not always that extraordinary. Sometimes you feel a simple invitation to relax and rest inside of the dynamic unity you are sharing. Other times, the contact is infused with depth and intensity, or tenderness and visions. It's unpredictable but reliably powerful.

Physical touch is another powerful form of contact, and not just between lovers. We've all heard stories or maybe even had experiences of people who are able to heal and release pain with a simple touch.

Often, we find that through one of the five senses it is easier to make contact with others. A powerful example is contained in Helen Keller's book *The World I Live In,* wherein she describes her experience of touch in a chapter entitled "The Seeing Hand":

> *I have just touched my dog. He was rolling in the grass with pleasure in every muscle and limb. I wanted to catch a picture of him with my fingers, and I touched him as lightly as I would cobwebs; but lo, his fat body revolved, stiffened, and solidified into an upright position and his tongue gave my hand a lick! He pressed close to me as if fain, he were to crowd himself into my hand. He loved it with his tail, with his paw, with his tongue. If he could speak, I believe he would say with me that paradise is attained by touch; for in touch is all love and intelligence.*[1]

Keller also describes how she connected with others by touching their hands. She could feel their character, their sense of aliveness, nervousness, joy, intelligence, and what she called "whimsy." Without access to sight and sound, the intensity and richness of her sense of touch was acutely developed.

All of us can experience this heightened sense of contact with others and the world around us if we work on awakening our essence through our senses. Usually, our attention is devoted to more dense and superficial layers of reality, which is why we miss clues and cues of what's possible between us. The physical senses are doorways to the more subtle dimensions through which our souls can come into contact. As we learn to stay alert to the experience of contact, we open ourselves up to a much deeper sensitivity. We also find that such contact is natural and available to us as human beings, though it requires our invitation and attention.

Sexual Contact

If you desire an Evolutionary Relationship with a sexual partner, then sexuality will be a primary source of contact. Erotic energy is the most direct and powerful expression of the evolutionary impulse, called *eros* by the ancient Greeks. This is the energy that creates life on all levels, from the basic act of physical procreation to the highest experience of divine union.

There are a multitude of teachings, moral laws, books, and perspectives on sexuality and the use of sexual energy. My intention in writing this book is not to overly focus on this dimension, because the potential I call Evolutionary Relationships is not limited to partnerships that include sexual intimacy. But since we are speaking about contact, it is important to consider this aspect of our relationships. It is one of the most primal and powerful ways that we can touch each other.

Looking back to Chapter One where we discussed Maslow's Hierarchy of Needs, it is relevant to note that the expression of sexuality changes at different levels of the pyramid. At the lowest survival levels, sexuality is pure instinct — a powerful and unconscious animal drive to ensure that the species endures. Moving up the pyramid, sex also can be a source of safety and security, since it can feed our self-esteem by making us feel desirable. It also can be a potent form of self-expression, particularly in cultures that allow us the freedom to explore our sexuality. In rare cases, sexuality can be a vehicle for self-transcendence, as in the ancient Tantric spiritual path which uses sexual engagement as a means to transcend the ego.

In our culture, much of our engagement with sexuality occurs at the level of self-esteem, and it often is driven by unconscious instinct. We see each other as sexually desirable objects that we seek in order to have a particular experience. Women are especially familiar with being seen this way, even more so if they fit the cultural standard of "attractiveness." In this way, sexuality is not a form of real contact, but a form of objectification that actually prevents contact at an essential level.

I remember once working with an extraordinarily beautiful film actress who was exhausted by and ready to give up on men. She told me that they would fall in love with her and pursue her with a passion — flying her to exotic places, buying her gifts, and wooing her in romantic ways. They truly believed they were in love with her, but when she moved in with them or married them, within months they were no longer interested in her sexually. The image of her that they held in their minds would wear off and they would discover that they weren't actually attracted to the woman she really was.

While most of us won't experience the heartache this beautiful actress experienced, we all know what it feels like to be objectified or to objectify another and fall in love with an image instead of discovering who is really there. When you enter into an Evolutionary Relationship with a sexual partner — whether it's someone you've been intimate with for many years or someone you recently met — you have the opportunity to discover who your partner really is and what is possible between you. The Eight Activating Principles we've been exploring are exactly what is needed to turn your relationship into a sacred marriage, a spiritual union. Then your sexual relationship will become an expression of profound contact at the deepest level.

In romantic relationships, when essential love is expressed physically through *eros* or alignment with the evolutionary impulse, the chemistry is endless. We are told that sexual passion dissipates over time, but that only happens when the passion is triggered from a more instinctual or egoic level. Real contact with *eros* and each other results in a different kind of passion where the fire never burns out. With this type of energy, you have to learn to withstand the level of intensity and pure beauty that comes through you both. The urgency of *eros* is felt as a demand to be with your beloved completely, always. To be separated by time or space feels intolerable and impossible. You become a force of love and life that encompasses wanting, giving, and receiving in one dynamic expression. As Cynthia Bourgeault writes:

> *Erotic love is a holy gift of God. And sometimes this love is so intense and powerful, and the sense of union so strong, that it continues right on growing beyond the grave, knitting two souls into the one wholeness they were always intended to become. Mystical completion does occur from time to time in our human experience and when it does, it bears witness to those two profound insights at the heart of Christian faith: that love is stronger than death, and that it is the fundamental creative force in the universe.*[2]

When two souls make love from this state of passion and union, there is an intuitive sense that what flows through you is a sacred energy that somehow benefits much more than just you and your partner. This lived experience of ecstatic union is a blessing, a gift to you and from you. It can be felt as the Divine loving itself through the two of you.

Such love speaks to a deep and passionate place in our souls — a place that recognizes that even one moment of this level of contact is worth any sacrifice. It reminds me of the movie *City of Angels*, where Nicholas Cage's character, who is an angel, chooses to fall from eternity to be with his human beloved. We see this archetype played out in many myths and stories, both ancient and modern.

Erotic love at this heightened level is quite beautiful, but it also can be very intense and hard to navigate. The most important preparation for this kind of contact is to practice the forms of mutual awakening we've been exploring in this book. Spiritually, we need to awaken together and experience the depth of who we are in contact with others. A sacred connection cannot be forced; it must be allowed to unfold on a physical level. Rather than becoming preoccupied with the contact, it is best to prepare and develop ourselves for the gift in the manner I've been describing — then you will be ready for the gift if it is given.

Of course, there are other expressions of divine love that are non-sexual and can be experienced as sweetness, compassion, warmth, joy, freedom, melting, kindness, and much more. But in a sexual relationship, there is the opportunity to also experience the release of passionate, ecstatic, erotic love. Everything can be given and received with nothing held back: your body, your emotions, day-to-day life, and dreams for the future.

If you are in an intimate relationship and you want to deepen the sexual contact, it's really not that complicated. Begin with the Mutual Awakening Practice, and make sure that you adopt an attitude of letting go of the need for any particular outcome. There's no orgasm to achieve, nothing specific that needs to happen. Then deepen the practice as lovers and see what unfolds. Stay acutely in the moment, allowing whatever is there (or not there) to be as it is. Be with each other, stay open and curious, and give fully to whatever can be shared.

You and your partner may experience a winding road at first, so it's important not to draw any definitive conclusions from whatever unfolds. Simply discover what is there. If natural chemistry exists between you, it will ignite and deepen. If your attraction and love has existed more in the realm of images and objectification, you may discover that you are more suited to be companions than lovers. As we've discussed, you need to be courageous to discover the truth of the relationship, even if it means the nature of partnership needs to shift. It is better to allow the relationship to shift than to hold on to an unconscious coupling that looks stable but is actually brittle and separate.

Most spiritual work focuses on solo realization. However, mutual awakening opens up new potentials for relationships: the union of two souls, becoming one being in conscious love, interpenetrating each other with radical intimacy. The exchange in an Evolutionary Relationship is complete and profound. It can build a level of connection and an inner abiding union that lasts beyond death.

Mental Contact

Mental contact is another beautiful domain to explore together. There will be certain people with whom you naturally connect at the level of ideas and intellectual discourse. Often, our mental exchanges are expressions of our egos — in order to reaffirm our self-image, we subtly (or not so subtly) expound our views and opinions with the intention of convincing another person to agree with us. The ego is full of fixed beliefs and perspectives that come from past experiences and conclusions. It is deeply invested in these mental constructs and in a more egoic intellectual conversation. It wants to be right, and it will defensively reinforce ideas that support the chosen self image. However, to make real contact on the mental level, we need to be open, in the present and, most importantly, in touch with our essence.

True contact happens when we exchange ideas and mutually explore the intellectual domain. Only then do we have access to each other's wisdom, insight, and brilliance. We also gain access to a higher mind that is bigger than both of us. When our mental contact is free from ego boundaries, the field of universal intelligence opens and we experience whatever the universe wishes to reveal about itself in and through us. It's like a hole opens up in the sky! Of course, the insights, ideas, creativity, and revelations that arise through us will be determined by the particular essence of each person and shaped by the knowledge and understandings we have developed in our lives.

My sense is that the great philosophers and their students shared this domain of contact. I like to imagine Plato and Aristotle sitting together in an ancient Greek temple and communing with a higher mind. Or picture Ralph Waldo Emerson, Henry David Thoreau, Walt Whitman, and their fellow transcendentalists sharing the thrill of new insights and perspectives in a pastoral New England setting.

Mental contact is the unique province of philosophers and partners in Evolutionary Relationships. The field of universal intelligence is available to all of us and it is enhanced when mutually shared with a partner.

We don't have to be philosophers to share exceptional mental contact in our relationships. We simply need to be present in our essence and remain open to each other. By listening deeply and staying open to touch, higher consciousness will awaken and begin to move through our conversations. The key is to be aware of how the ego will try to hijack such moments through insistence on its opinions and old assumptions. If you allow the ego to have a voice in the conversation, it will undermine the experience of openness and contact. But if you can hold the ego at bay, you will discover natural intuitive capacities, illumination, subtle perceptions, revelation, prophetic awareness, and even access to what could be called omniscience — the ability to tap into universal knowledge, simply by turning your consciousness toward direct knowing.

One of the ways to activate contact in the higher mind is to begin with a question that both of you are truly excited to explore together with open-ended inquiry. Hold the question between you and see what ideas, images, and sensations begin to arise. Share the revelations and see where they take you. It's best not to seek any answer. A novel question and genuine curiosity will give you access to an exciting world of contact.

Emotional and Energetic Contact

Emotional contact is much more than simply expressing or sharing our feelings with each other. When we come into contact at a soul level, we become attuned to each other's emotional and energetic currents without necessarily having to speak about them. The word "attune" means to bring into harmony, and this is how it feels to be in contact at an emotional level — a sensitive dance of attention and interchange that happens between two people when they tune into each other. Psychotherapist Richard Erskine defines attunement this way:

> *A kinesthetic and emotional sensing of others, knowing their rhythm, affect and experience by metaphorically being in their skin, and going beyond empathy to create a two-person experience of unbroken feeling connectedness by providing a reciprocal affect and/or resonating response.*[3]

Attunement is a skill we can develop together. We can learn how to tune in to each other, just as a radio can be tuned to a particular frequency. In a sense, all the material contained in this book contributes to developing our capacity to be attuned to ourselves, to others, to the world, and even to other dimensions of existence. By developing these skills with a partner, we greatly increase our capacity to be attuned in all situations, including subtle domains that ordinarily are inaccessible.

Typically, most people are only aware of the surface situation, thereby missing the actual reality of what is present. When we touch each other in a normal state of consciousness, we move quickly and we aren't attuned to each other or to what really is happening.

True attunement, on the other hand, indicates a responsiveness to others that originates from a depth that allows us to experience the other person. To be attuned means that as you feel or sense the other person, you allow yourself to respond to where they are mentally, emotionally, spiritually, and physically. A natural self-regulation occurs because you are in contact with the deeper reality that exists in the moment with that person and your attuned response to them.

Be aware that as you gain access to new levels of consciousness, it takes more courage and compassion to live it. Your sense of attunement won't shut off. You might be in a business meeting and sense that your coworkers are avoiding deeper issues, even though nothing can move forward until those issues are addressed. At that moment, you can shine your awareness of what is really happening on the situation. It may not always be easy, but you will be more productive and powerful because you can make a difference in any situation in which you find yourself. I've found that if I share what I am seeing or sensing with openness and ask others if they sense it as well, the space opens and moves forward. It takes some boldness to address the reality of a room, but it is part of what we can contribute to each other when we are attuned.

As you enter into sustained Evolutionary Relationships, you may notice that you start to develop extraordinary capacities for sensing and knowing that are hard to explain. Attunement, as it deepens, leads to more and more mysterious capacities that allow us to be in contact with each other, even when we are not together physically. I call this the "innernet." As our sense of self relocates back to the core of our being and we identify less and less with our fixed and separate ego, we naturally become continuously available to our connection with others at an exceedingly deep level. After all, we are interconnected, and inside this kind of consciousness it becomes a lived reality.

For example, your intuition will increase. Your ability to "read a room" more completely and comprehensively also will expand. You may find it easier to enter into altered states of consciousness. You even may find that you have access to forms of extrasensory perception, which means a kind of sensing and access to information that is not channeled through the five physical senses. This can include clairvoyance (clear seeing), claircognizance (clear or direct knowing), clairauditory (clear hearing), clairsentience (clear feeling), and clairkinesthesia (clear touching). While these capacities have not been scientifically proven to exist, there is ample anecdotal evidence that humans have the potential to attune to much more information than our physical senses can show us. But don't take my word for it — simply be open and do the practices in this book. You then will discover for yourself that, as Hamlet said, "There are more things in heaven and earth ... than are dreamt of in your philosophy."*

Another capacity that may emerge as you move deeper into contact with another person is that you are able to communicate without using words or conventional means. Some people call this ability "telepathy," which means the transmission of information from one person to another without using a known sensory channel or physical interaction. Whatever term we use, I think this ability is a natural extension of our human capacity for empathy — our ability to feel what another person is feeling. I sometimes refer to this capacity as "telepathic empathy," which I define as the ability to deeply feel, sense, and understand people on multiple levels.

Normally, we are trained to distance ourselves, not only from others but from our own deeper feelings and intuitions. When we establish Evolutionary Relationships and become more intimate and sensitive, we open up channels of access we didn't know existed. Telepathic empathy is not limited by time or space. That's why Peter could sense my pain more than half a world away. As our consciousness expands, we also find that time becomes fluid. Even information about the past can be accessed, and we also may divine emergent potentials of the future.

It's been my experience, and the experience of many people I've worked with, that when we begin to dwell in the intersubjective, interrelated world of true contact, our circuits open to these extrasensory capacities. It's not necessarily that we suddenly have access to these channels, but if something important happens with our partner or in the field we share, we will know it immediately. It's like getting an alert or an urgent text, and it may come in the form of a feeling, an image, or an impulse to make contact. Many people experience this innernet, especially when something dire occurs with a partner or loved one.

Today, the debate continues as to whether these so-called psychic powers are real. Thus far, science has found little if any conclusive evidence. However, if we look at how our miraculous universe works and at how new capacities and potentials come into being through the course of evolution, it doesn't seem far-fetched to imagine that abilities which now appear "superhuman" might one day simply be "human." Perhaps in time this innernet will become as natural and obvious to us as our ability to communicate across vast distances through the internet. Remember, one hundred years ago, the communication capacities we have today would have sounded like science fiction.

The glimpses we get of advanced human capacities for contact may be precursors of what the future holds for us. One day, I predict the innernet will become a natural form of consciousness as humanity moves into shared unity consciousness. Certainly, my good friend Barbara Marx Hubbard believes such grand human capacities are just over the horizon. Furthermore, as the great science fiction writer William Gibson quipped, "The future is here. It's just not very evenly distributed."[5]

As you practice and delve into Evolutionary Relationships, you are the pioneers of this new emerging consciousness. I encourage you to become more deeply attuned to yourself, to others, and to the world around you. If you follow the practices in this book, you will find — as I and many of my students and close friends have found — that these capacities are normal, natural, and incredibly useful. They represent ways in which we can come more deeply into contact with each other, unhindered by the barriers of separation, ego, and superficial realities.

EXERCISE:
Make Contact

Step 1. One of the simplest practices for opening the connection between two people starts with sitting across from each other at a close but comfortable distance. You may want to try moving closer and farther away from each other to see how proximity affects your sense of being together and ability to connect. My advice is to err on the side of sitting closer than your normal social-self would choose. Although you may feel shy or a bit embarrassed to be so close, proximity to each other will enhance this exercise.

Step 2. When you've found your optimal distance, close your eyes. Center yourself, and then expand your awareness to include the other.

Step 3. Now open your eyes and take a few moments to get comfortable, without saying any words or any distractions. Look into your partner's eyes — first at your partner's right eye and then at their left eye. Notice if their eyes feel different to you (often they do). Then choose one eye to focus on (otherwise you can end up tracking your partner's eyes, which will be distracting for your partner).

Step 4. Relax and be present and open. Mentally invite your partner to be present with you as well. Don't try to make anything happen or not happen. Simply focus on your partner — seeing him or her and being open to who they are. If you get distracted by thoughts, refocus on the color of your partner's eye or its shape, so that you remain emotionally present and spiritually engaged. Continue like this for 5 minutes and then close your eyes for 1 minute, allowing yourself to feel where you are with your partner.

Step 5: Open your eyes again and repeat Step 4. You can do this cycle two or three times. Then share with your partner how this level of contact felt and what arose for you during the session. ✆

For supplementary content, including audios, videos, and exercises, visit: www.EvolutionaryRelationshipsBook.com/bonus

Notes

1 Helen Keller, *The World I Live In*, New York, NY: The Century Co., 1908, pp. 3-4.

2 Cynthia Bourgeault, *Love Is Stronger Than Death: The Mystical Union of Two Souls*, Great Barrington, MA: SteinerBooks, 2001.

3 Richard Erksine, *Relational Patterns, Therapeutic Presence: Concepts and Practice of Integrative Psychotherapy*, London, UK: Karnac Books, 2015, p. 45.

4 William Shakespeare, *Hamlet* (1.5.167-8), Hamlet to Horatio.

5 William Gibson, in an interview on *Fresh Air*, NPR, August 31, 1993.

EPILOGUE
Evolving Relatedness

I hope that by reading this book and engaging in the practices I've shared, you have tasted a new potential for human relatedness. If so, you and your partner have sensed a heightened "we-space" and connected to something much greater than your individual selves.

This potential for Evolutionary Relationships that I've been describing is not merely about forming a better friendship or marriage. And the Eight Activating Principles we have been working with are not simply tools to improve our interpersonal skills. As we enter into this new way of being together, we discover that it's not about "me" … it's not even about "us." It's about the "WEvolution" — which represents the cutting edge of consciousness. By practicing this simple and very human way of relating, we become one with the vastness of the evolving process of which we are all a part.

In the opening chapter, I reflected on how our global culture is becoming more and more complex and interconnected. I suggested that we are a "crossover generation" and that we are becoming, in a real sense, a new form of human being with a new kind of consciousness. The name of our species, *Homo sapiens sapiens*, defines us as the species that knows itself, that is self-aware. Futurists have even come up with names for the new species that may be emerging. Barbara Marx Hubbard calls it the Universal Human or *Homo universalis*, Pierre Teilhard de Chardin used the term *Homo progressivus*, and John White uses *Homo noeticus*. Whatever name we adopt, I believe it will reflect the defining characteristic of the new human: a species with awareness not only of itself but also of a global and even universal connectedness. The new human's consciousness will be multidimensional, easily encompassing simultaneous awareness of self, other, we, and more. The locus of our awareness will be inclusive, fluid, and rich.

Futurists seem to agree that the new human will be less individualistic and that our sense of self will arise from and be rooted in unity consciousness. Consequently, we will have the experience of being part of the matrix of a larger design of reality, guided by higher wisdom in concert with others. Personal uniqueness will not be lost in the expansion to this wider awareness. Rather, our sense of self will become more distinct and illuminated as a deeper relatedness is shared between us and is seen as an essential contribution to the purpose of the whole.

> *I believe mutual awakening is the key to our continued evolution and our very survival. I also believe that Evolutionary Relationships are a prerequisite for co-creating a universal consciousness for all humanity.*

The great Austrian mystic Eva Pierrakos, who gave a series of lectures in the 1950s that are known today as the Pathwork, described mutuality as a cosmic principle. "No creation can take place unless mutuality exists," she said. "Mutuality means that two apparently or superficially different entities or aspects move toward one another for the purpose of uniting and making one comprehensive whole."[1] I agree. Mutuality, as she describes it, is much more than a human experience. It is an inherently creative state of being that collectively connects us to the driving force behind our ever-expanding cosmos.

When we practice coming together with this knowledge in mind, our human relationships become what Teilhard de Chardin described as "creative unions" — connections that bring into being something that did not exist before. As we turn toward each other using the Activating Principles — engagement, commitment, truth, trust, openness, uniqueness, influence, and contact — the space between us is catalyzed and we are in fact enacting the work of evolution. Deeper relatedness not only is where evolution is moving, but the very process by which it progresses.

Additionally, Teilhard pointed out that creative unions are formed through the exchange of what he called "characteristic energy." This energy is what allows holonic parts to make connections with each other; it also forms the bond between them. Beatrice Bruteau, a Teilhardian scholar, further describes the next creative union that is forming between human beings. She writes that a "New Being" is emerging "from the connections and interactions of the composing units, and it constitutes a new level of oneness and wholeness."[2] She also points out that while evolution always progresses via the process of union, with atoms coming together to form molecules and molecules forming cells and so forth, there now is a critical difference.

> At this point, evolution meets a situation that is unique in its history: the uniting elements, in our case, are free agents. ... Thus the union, the New Being, the next creative advance of evolution, will come about only if we freely consent to form it.[3]

This conscious decision to become new humans is why each individual and every relationship is so important at this moment in human history. Without our conscious commitment and engagement, a more enlightened future cannot emerge. We need to consciously choose to come together and exchange a new modality of relating — a new characteristic energy that will bond us together at a higher level.

The characteristic energy normally shared by human beings is what I've been describing in this book as "egoic." It is the energy of separation, competition, self-concern, selfishness, protectiveness, fear, deception, deficiency, and aggression. It also can be colored by various projections, both positive and negative. Typically, we also exchange the energy of desire, basic survival instincts, sexuality, and social connections. There is nothing wrong with normal energetic exchange, but it will not give us access to the opening that is ahead of us — the possibility to engage consciously on a higher level and create a "new being." Our choice to give ourselves to this endeavor should be seen with the importance that it truly holds.

Increasing numbers of people are being drawn to consciously come together and share the characteristic energy of truth, love, authenticity, and our essential nature. Such gatherings need to include a mutual commitment to be in an ongoing relationship with each other. We may be introduced to higher levels of consciousness through a book such as this, a weekend workshop, or shared spiritual practices, but to actually create the necessary energetic networks of the future, we need to focus, commit, and practice mutual awakening over the long term.

The leading edge of evolution is consciousness itself, and our collective awakening is where energy and focus is needed. By consistently using the practices in this book and, more importantly, by aligning with and mastering the Activating Principles in our relationships, we help promote the conscious evolution of our world.

Spiritual awakening is evolving as well. In the past, religious traditions generally focused on self-realization through solo practices of prayer, meditation, and study. Working with a spiritual teacher or guru has been standard fare for thousands of years. At this point in our evolution, however, the path to unity consciousness has taken on new meaning and new urgency.

Today, unity consciousness does not simply mean connecting to Source. It also means connecting from our deepest center to the center of another human being. As we do so, the depth and possibility for two souls to be united in conscious love points to a new spirituality — the spirituality of group awakening and multiple Beloveds. The potential for many people coming together as collectives and exploring unity consciousness will be the focus of my next book in the WEvolution series.

All the progress and wonderment surrounding mutual (two people) and collective (group) awakening makes me wonder: *How far can we new humans take our innate desire to come together? How much evolutionary progress will we achieve once we unleash our natural desire for intimacy and connection?*

Your origination point is naturally attracted to its counterpart in the other. When you do the Mutual Awakening Practice, there will be times when you feel yourself powerfully drawn to your partner in a way that is indescribably rich. The intensity of love in Evolutionary Relationships will feel like the force of gravity. In my own experience of sharing this process with many people, I can see the larger movement that is occurring as we become more aligned and capable of connecting center-to-center. There is a palpable quality of unification, like neurons hooking up in the brain, except that *we* are the neurons. We are becoming a unified collective with capacities and potentials we cannot yet imagine.

One of the most eloquent descriptions of this unification I have ever heard came from a man named Igal, who participated in a virtual class I taught. Igal did the Mutual Awakening Practice with a stranger on the phone and later shared this reflection on his experience:

> *The space in between us became vivid and enlivened. As I continued exploring, leaning into it more and more, it became this vortex of consciousness, which had a momentum of its own. It was very compelling and had almost a kind of "sucking in" momentum that was changing the experience of self, my sense of self, from someone limited in my body (kind of a consciousness inhabiting a body) to, in this case, two bodies being consumed by a vortex of consciousness. Being two was secondary to the incredible oneness of the consciousness that consumed us.*

Another powerful example comes from Gail, one of the Evolutionary Collective members who happens to be a Catholic nun. Gail told me that she was able to activate and experience an evolutionary connection with a group of nuns she was training in Peru.

> *There was such depth and expansiveness shared in the space between us. Love exploded as the group broke through gravity and tore through separation consciousness into the unity of the Field. The sisters had been working a bit on the new consciousness and definitely have a cosmological perspective, but this gathering far surpassed anything anyone, even myself, could have imagined.*

The presence of the heart of Christ was a Blazing Fire filling the space, demanding everything from each and all of us, and there was such desire to jump into this heart, this Conflagration, together. The sisters went as far as they could toward that searing, burning edge and dipped in. Even as I write these words, I could just weep with the beauty and profundity of it all.

I have heard countless more examples of experiences like this, both from people engaged in my work and from others who work with similar principles. Every time I hear such testimonies, I feel the same powerful drive echoing through their words — the energy of evolution itself drawing us together. The WEvolution is beginning to find its way into our awareness. I have no doubt that this is what we are here to do, in the midst of this fast-changing, complexifying, and exhilarating time in history.

Mystical communion is available as we work with the Activating Principles. It allows us to open ourselves to the movement of love and grace that takes us directly into the heart of the cosmos. Evolution is calling us to catalyze and embody this next stage of human development. We are being supported to come together beyond ego to reach new potentials for love, creativity, and collective action. We begin to function not as a group of individuals with competing ideas and agendas trying to get something done, but more like a jazz quartet, improvising and flowing as one body. That's where I believe we are headed.

Evolution has taken us from the first spark of self-awareness through an extraordinary journey of individuation and personal development. Now, the edge of human consciousness is moving toward a more advanced human with the consciousness of absorption, spontaneity, flow, intimacy, and immediacy. This may sound far-fetched or idealistic, but I'm sure you've already had glimpses of it. Think of a time when you were in a "flow" state, fully self-expressed while completely in a dance with others and with life. We assume this kind of heightened consciousness is temporary and fleeting. Clearly it is not a stable state for most human beings, yet that doesn't mean we aren't headed in this direction. More and more people are beginning to study and pay attention to the extraordinary capacities that come online when we move into higher states of consciousness.

In the same way, I imagine that in the early stages of human evolution, the capacity for self-awareness didn't arise full-blown. A few early humans probably had moments of self-reflection and then went back into unthinking, instinctual behavior. Later in our development, the moments of self-awareness lasted a little longer and happened more frequently, until eventually, self-reflective consciousness became part of our birthright as human beings.

Those of you who are reading this book are the pioneers, the innovators, the ones in whom the first glimmer of this longing for unity consciousness is arising. Your feelings of discontent with our current modes of human relating constitute the sparks of potential that will transform not just you but humanity itself. This potential reveals itself subtly at first, as a vague sense that something just doesn't feel right. Then, as you follow your intuition and longing, you will discover that the forces of evolution are moving through you — calling you and calling all of us to awaken to a new way of being together.

You are invited, by reading and using the principles shared in this book, to continue the sacred journey you already have commenced. I promise you, if you give yourself fully to the evolutionary impulse, it will take you to the farthest reaches of love.

Notes

1   Eva Pierrakos, "Mutuality: A Cosmic Principle and Law," Pathwork Guide Lecture No. 185, October 9, 1970, http://pathwork.org/lectures/mutuality-a-cosmic-principle-and-law.

2   Beatrice Bruteau interviewed by Amy Edelstein, July 13, 2013, http://amyedelstein.com/evolutionary-spirituality-beatrice-bruteau.

3   Ibid.

ABOUT THE AUTHOR

Patricia Albere is an internationally known contemporary spiritual teacher, author, and founder of the Evolutionary Collective. She has worked with over 200,000 people in groups during the past 40 years, pioneering the new fields of intersubjective awakening and post-personal development.

Albere guides people to move beyond introspection and the quest for solo enlightenment into the more challenging work of mutual awakening and unity consciousness. She calls this field of advanced relatedness the "we space" in which Evolutionary Relationships are possible. She believes that higher order relatedness is the essential next stage of human evolution — a collective state of being shared by larger and larger groups of people. Ultimately, she envisions a "WEvolution" that inspires humanity to reach far beyond the limits of ego, separation, and self-improvement, into a new awareness of our oneness and shared potentials.

It all started in 1971, when Albere found herself at the leading edge of the human potential movement, as an original member of the EST organization (currently, Landmark Education). Working with cultural icon and transformational movement pioneer, Werner Erhard, Albere played an important role in expanding EST's global reach and training the organization's leaders. Albere's work with Erhard laid the foundation for her passionate commitment to facilitating real transformation, which she asserts is at the heart of what makes human life meaningful: "Real transformation means that a person's life is irrevocably changed in a way that empowers them to fulfill their highest potentials."

By age thirty-three, Albere was highly revered as a public speaker, transformational teacher, and workshop leader. It was then that her inquiry into human transformation was catapulted to an entirely new level due to a profound personal relationship that forever changed her. A chance meeting with the man who would become her partner of four years opened up new experiential pathways for Albere to discover the potential of sacred intimacy and the inter-communion of two souls. Through this new way of being together, Albere experienced a mutual awakening with her partner which catalyzed and compelled her to pursue this work.

"For the first time I experienced the limitless potential that exists between two human beings," says Albere. "We pushed the boundaries of love, moving through all the challenges that arise in any relationship, while traversing previously untapped potentials of our own consciousness. And from there, I was shown a new paradigm of relating that was possible for all human beings."

Albere's awakening to this new form of relatedness placed her at the forefront of an emerging spiritual and cultural movement. "It's a really exciting time for humanity to explore what's possible in all forms of relationship," says Albere, "because it's the action of coming together that allows us to push beyond the edges of our own personal growth and liberation into a truly inspired and expansive unknown by way of authentic relatedness, mutuality, and love."

In 2007, Patricia created the Evolutionary Collective to gather together those who are ready to engage in this next evolutionary stage of human development. Many people are aware that we need a new consciousness equipped for the Information Age — an "innernet" that allows us to live from a powerful field of interconnectedness. The Evolutionary Collective is building a global society of people who are developing a shared unity consciousness that is necessary to navigate this new world.

Visit the Evolutionary Collective website to learn more about Patricia's work and to receive a free download of her ebook *Mutual Awakening*.

www.EvolutionaryCollective.com
www.PatriciaAlbere.com

ABOUT THE PUBLISHER

Oracle Institute Press is the award-winning publishing house of The Oracle Institute, a 501(c)(3) educational charity whose mission is to foster interfaith unity, promote sacred activism, and build a new world based on shared moral values and a culture of peace.

Oracle Press publishes books about humanity's quest for Truth, Love, and Light, including texts on the world's great religions and wisdom traditions, the arts, education, and more. To date, our press has garnered five prestigious book awards in categories such as religion, spirituality, children's fiction, and the performing arts.

Oracle Press works closely with authors to co-create beautiful, relevant, and impactful books published under the Oracle imprint. Our non-profit press also offers a wide spectrum of services to authors who wish to self-publish when the project is aligned with the educational mission of The Oracle Institute.

To learn more about Oracle Press, visit:
www.TheOracleInstitute.org/Press

To shop at our online bookstore, visit:
www.TheOracleInstitute.org/Store

And to learn more about the mission of The Oracle Institute or
to participate in our other programs and activities,
we invite you to visit our community at the Oracle Campus:

The Oracle Institute

Peace Pentagon
88 Oracle Way
Independence, VA 24348

www.TheOracleInstitute.org